When **Sally** Met **Kanban**

Experience Kanban through a captivating story

Manav Agarwal

Copyright © 2024 Manav Agarwal

All rights reserved.

ISBN: 9798340823427

PREFACE

When I set out to write this book, When Kanban Met Sally, my goal was simple: to make learning Kanban feel less like reading a manual and more like following a relatable, engaging story. Too often, guidebooks can feel dry, rigid, and disconnected from our day-to-day lives. I wanted to change that. I wanted to create something that resonates with people on a personal level—something that makes you nod your head in recognition, maybe chuckle at the similarities to your own experiences, and leave you feeling more confident and inspired to implement Kanban.

The idea behind this book is to bring storytelling to guidebooks in a way that feels real and practical. Whether you're new to Kanban or just looking for a fresh perspective, Sally's journey will guide you through the core concepts and help you see how Kanban can fit into your own workflow. The power of storytelling lies in its ability to make even the most complex concepts digestible and relatable. By following Sally's ups and downs, I hope you'll find yourself immersed in the story while learning valuable lessons along the way.

Now, you'll notice that each chapter ends with a section called Manav's Thoughts. This is where I take a step back from the story to share more advanced insights, discuss key Kanban concepts in greater depth, and recommend resources for further exploration. If you're looking to build a foundational understanding of Kanban, feel free to focus primarily on the story. But if you want a more holistic view—one that not only introduces you to the basics but also encourages you to dive deeper into the methodology—then I highly recommend you spend some time in the Manav's Thoughts sections.

However you choose to read this book, whether you immerse yourself fully in both the story and the thoughts sections, or you skip ahead to focus on just the basics, I'm confident you'll come away with a strong understanding of Kanban and how it can transform your workflow.

This book is for anyone who has ever felt overwhelmed by their workload, for those who are searching for a better way to manage the chaos, and for those who are curious about how to optimize the flow of work—whether in their professional life or beyond.

I'm truly excited to share this journey with you, and I hope that as you follow Sally's path, you'll find inspiration, practical knowledge, and maybe even a few laughs along the way. Thank you for picking up this book. I believe it will not only help you learn Kanban but also inspire you to approach your work with a fresh perspective.

Happy reading, and welcome to the world of Kanban!

Warm regards,

Manav

Contents

The Treadmill of Chaos ... 1

The Kanban Kerfuffle ... 11

A Glimmer of Hope ... 21

Kanban 101: Seeing the Work ... 29

Stop Starting, Start Finishing ... 37

Pull, Don't Push ... 47

Smooth Operator: Optimizing Flow ... 57

Feedback Loops: The Key to Continuous Improvement ... 65

Expanding Horizons: Kanban Beyond the Team ... 77

The Customer Connection ... 87

Kanban 2.0: Advanced Techniques ... 97

The Kanban Mindset Shift ... 107

A Year in the Life of a Kanban Team ... 117

ACKNOWLEDGMENT

This book is the result of countless interactions, experiences and insights I've gained through an incredible community of Agile practitioners and enthusiasts.

First of all, my heartfelt thanks go to all the participants in my Agile workshops and courses. Your questions, arising from the unique challenges of your teams and industries, have been the cornerstone of my growing understanding of Kanban. Whether in healthcare, finance, public administration or start-ups, your diverse perspectives have led me to explore the versatility of this framework and find new, innovative ways to apply it in different areas. You are the co-creators of this book and have shaped it with every question like "But how does it work in our industry?".

A huge thank you goes out to all the tech teams I have had the honor of working with. As an Agile Coach, Product Owner and Scrum Master, I have been lucky enough to be part of your journeys. Your successes have been my successes, your challenges my learning moments. This book is as much a product of your experiences as my words.

To my customers who had the courage to embark on the path of agile transformation with me - your trust was my greatest motivation. Your willingness to question the status quo, embrace change and relentlessly strive for improvement has been an inexhaustible source of inspiration. The stories in this book reflect your courage and determination.

A very special thank you to my family and friends who patiently endured my endless analogies on a daily basis and supported me through the ups and downs of the writing process. Your love and encouragement were my constant sprint goal.

Finally, I would like to thank you, the reader. By choosing to pick up this book, you are taking a step towards better understanding and applying Kanban. Whether you are a novice or an experienced Agile practitioner, I hope Sally's story speaks to you and enriches your Agile journey.

Thank you all for being part of this incredible Agile journey. This book was created for you and because of you.

Chapter 1

The Treadmill of Chaos

Sally McKinnon's bloodshot eyes flicked to the clock on her desk, its glowing digits taunting her: 7:23 AM. She'd already been at her desk for over an hour, gulping coffee that tasted more like desperation than caffeine. Her inbox swelled with unread messages, each one a ticking time bomb disguised as a polite subject line. The day hadn't even started, yet it loomed over her like an avalanche waiting to bury her alive.

"Just one more email," she muttered, reaching for her fourth cup of coffee. The bitter liquid had long since lost its taste, becoming nothing more than fuel for her overworked brain.

As she hit send on what felt like her hundredth email of the morning, a sticky note fluttered down from the mess surrounding her monitor. Sally snatched it out of the air, squinting at the hastily scrawled reminder: "Buy cat food!"

She groaned. Poor Schrödinger would have to survive on tuna tonight. Again. At this rate, her cat was more likely to see the inside of a can than she was to see the inside of a grocery store.

The sudden ping of an incoming message made her jump. It was from Dave, the lead developer, and it read simply: "Sally, we need to talk. ASAP."

Sally's stomach dropped. In her experience, nothing good ever followed those words, especially not from Dave. She took a deep breath, straightened her rumpled blouse, and made her way to the development team's corner of the office.

Dave's desk was a mirror image of her own — a chaos of papers, sticky notes, and empty energy drink cans. The developer himself looked like he hadn't slept in days, his usual disheveled appearance amplified to new heights.

"Morning, Dave," Sally said, trying to inject some cheer into her voice. "What's the emergency?"

Dave looked up at her, his eyes wide with a mix of panic and caffeine-induced mania. "The payment gateway integration. It's... it's not working."

Sally felt her forced smile falter. "What do you mean, 'not working'? We've been working on that for weeks. The demo for the client is tomorrow!"

Dave ran a hand through his hair, somehow making it stand up even more. "I mean, it's rejecting every transaction we try to process. I've been here all night trying to fix it, but..." He trailed off, gesturing helplessly at his screen.

Sally squinted at the screen, the wall of text blurring into incomprehensible hieroglyphs. To her, code might as well have been an ancient spellbook, its incantations entirely indecipherable. Still, she forced herself to exhale slowly. "Alright, Dave," she said, her voice steadier than she felt. "Have you looped in Tina? She's got an eye for spotting these things."

Dave's laugh was hollow, a sound borne of exhaustion. "Tina? She's drowning in the bug backlog. Unless she's sprouted an extra pair of arms, we're on our own."

As if summoned by her name, Tina appeared behind them, looking harried. "Did I hear my name? Please tell me you're not adding another item to my queue. I'm drowning here!"

Sally turned to face the QA specialist, taking in her frazzled appearance. Tina's usually neat ponytail was coming undone, and there were dark circles under her eyes that rivaled Sally's own.

"Tina, I know you're swamped, but we've got a critical issue with the payment gateway. Is there any way you could take a look?"

Tina's eyes widened in horror. "The payment gateway? But that's supposed to go live tomorrow! What happened?"

As Dave launched into a technical explanation that went way over Sally's head, she felt her phone vibrate in her pocket. Pulling it out, she saw a message from Alex, their UX designer: "Where are you??? The client meeting for the new dashboard design started 5 minutes ago!"

Sally's heart rate spiked. How could she have forgotten about that meeting? She'd been so focused on putting out fires that she'd completely lost track of her schedule.

"I've got to go," she interrupted Dave mid-sentence. "Client meeting. Tina, please, if you can spare even an hour to help Dave, I'd owe you big time. Dave, keep working on it, and I'll check back as soon as I'm done with this meeting."

Without waiting for a response, Sally rushed towards the conference room, her mind racing. How was she going to explain the payment gateway issue to the client? Should she even mention it, or hope they could fix it before tomorrow's demo?

She burst into the conference room, slightly out of breath, to find Alex sitting alone with their client, Brad from marketing. Alex shot her a look that was equal parts relief and annoyance.

"Sally! There you are," Brad said, his enthusiasm undimmed by her tardiness. "We were just discussing some exciting new ideas for the dashboard!"

Sally plastered on her best professional smile as she took a seat. "Sorry I'm late, got held up with a... technical issue. What have I missed?"

As Alex began to recap the conversation, Sally's mind wandered. She thought about the mountain of unread emails waiting for her, the impending disaster of the payment gateway, Tina's overflowing bug queue, and the fact that she still needed to buy cat food. How had things gotten this out of control?

The meeting dragged on, with Brad suggesting increasingly outlandish features for the dashboard. "What if we added a 3D visualization that users could manipulate with VR gloves?" he asked excitedly.

Sally exchanged a weary glance with Alex. They both knew that implementing even half of Brad's ideas would push their already strained resources to the breaking point. But how could they say no to the client?

As Alex tried to gently steer Brad towards more realistic options, Sally's phone buzzed again. A message from Linda, their project manager: "Need update on payment gateway ASAP. CEO asking questions."

Sally felt a bead of sweat form on her forehead. This was quickly turning into a perfect storm of chaos. She needed to wrap up this meeting, check on Dave's progress, update Linda, and somehow find time to eat something more substantial than coffee and despair.

Finally, after what felt like hours, the meeting concluded. Brad left, brimming with excitement about his "revolutionary" new dashboard design. As soon as the door closed behind him, Alex slumped in his chair.

"That was... intense," he said, rubbing his temples. "How are we supposed to implement all of that? We're already behind on three other projects!"

Sally sighed. "I don't know, Alex. But right now, we've got bigger problems. The payment gateway integration is broken, and the demo is tomorrow."

Alex's eyes widened. "What? But that's our biggest feature! What are we going to do?"

"I don't know," Sally repeated, feeling the weight of their collective stress pressing down on her. "But we need to figure it out, fast."

As they left the conference room, they found the office in a state of barely controlled chaos. Dave was hunched over his keyboard, muttering to himself as his fingers flew across the keys. Tina had set up camp at a nearby desk, her own work forgotten as she helped troubleshoot the payment issue. Other team members were huddled in small groups, their voices hushed but urgent.

Sally's desk, when she finally made it back, was even more of a disaster than when she'd left it. New sticky notes had appeared, each bearing a message more urgent than the last. Her email inbox had exploded, the unread count now a number she was afraid to contemplate.

As she sank into her chair, Linda appeared, her usually composed demeanor showing cracks of concern. "Sally, I need that update on the payment gateway. The CEO is breathing down my neck."

Sally took a deep breath, trying to organize her thoughts. "It's... not good, Linda. Dave's been working on it all night, and Tina's helping now, but we're not sure what's causing the problem. I don't know if we'll have it fixed in time for tomorrow's demo."

Linda's face fell. "This is bad, Sally. Really bad. We've been hyping this feature for months. If we can't deliver..." She didn't need to finish the sentence. They both knew what was at stake.

As Linda walked away, presumably to deliver the bad news up the chain, Sally felt a wave of despair wash over her. How had they gotten to this point? When had their processes broken down so completely that they were constantly on the brink of disaster?

She thought back to her first days with the company, when everything had seemed so full of potential. They were going to revolutionize the industry, create amazing products, and have fun doing it. Now, it felt like they were barely keeping their heads above water.

The rest of the day passed in a blur of crisis management. Sally bounced between Dave and Tina, trying to help where she could and running interference with stakeholders when she couldn't. She fielded panicked calls from Brad about the dashboard design, reassured the CEO that they were doing everything possible to fix the payment gateway, and somehow managed to scarf down a stale granola bar she found in her desk drawer.

By the time 8 PM rolled around, Sally felt like she'd aged a decade. The payment gateway was still stubbornly broken, despite Dave and Tina's best efforts. The dashboard design was a mess of conflicting requirements and unrealistic expectations. And somewhere in the back of her mind, a small voice reminded her that Schrödinger was still waiting for his dinner.

As she gathered her things to leave, Sally caught sight of herself in the reflection of her darkened monitor. Her hair was a mess, her eyes were red-rimmed, and she looked about as far from a successful business analyst as one could get.

"There has to be a better way," she muttered to herself, not for the first time that day. But what? They'd tried so many different approaches over the years, each promising to be the silver bullet that would solve all their problems. None had lived up to the hype.

Sally's phone buzzed one last time as she was walking to her car. It was a calendar reminder for tomorrow: "9 AM - Payment Gateway Demo for Executive Team."

She stared at the screen for a long moment, then let out a bitter laugh. Tomorrow was going to be a disaster, and there was nothing she could do about it. Or was there?

As she drove home, her mind raced with possibilities. Maybe it was time for a radical change. Maybe they needed to throw out everything they thought they knew about project management and start from scratch.

By the time she pulled into her driveway, a plan was starting to form in Sally's mind. It was risky, potentially career-ending if it went wrong. But if it worked...

She walked into her house, greeted by the indignant meows of a hungry Schrödinger. As she opened a can of tuna for the disgruntled feline, Sally made a decision. Tomorrow, after the inevitable trainwreck of the demo, she was going to propose something crazy. Something that might just save their team from drowning in chaos.

Little did Sally know, her idea would set in motion a series of events that would change not just her team, but the entire company. The journey from chaos to flow was about to begin, and nothing would ever be the same again.

As she fell into bed that night, exhausted but oddly energized, Sally's last thought before sleep claimed her was simple: "Something has to change. And I'm going to be the one to change it."

Manav's Thoughts:

At this point in the story, Sally is struggling with unorganized tasks, constant interruptions, and unclear priorities. While the team hasn't yet implemented any formal process, the introduction of Work Item Types could already help them bring some clarity to their chaos.

Work Item Types refer to categorizing tasks based on their nature—e.g., bugs, features, technical debt, and experiments. Even before implementing Kanban, recognizing these categories can help teams understand what kind of work is consuming their time and whether they're focusing on the right areas.

By identifying different types of work early on, Sally's team could better prioritize what needs to be done, balancing their attention between immediate fixes (like bugs) and long-term goals (like feature development). This could also help with stakeholder communication, as they would have a clearer picture of how much work is focused on improving the product versus maintaining it.

From a practical standpoint, understanding work item types helps teams avoid falling into the trap of firefighting (e.g., focusing only on bug fixes) and can promote a more balanced approach to managing work.

For further reading on Work Item Types and their practical applications, I recommend:

- "Kanban: Successful Evolutionary Change for Your Technology Business" by David J. Anderson
- "Making Work Visible: Exposing Time Theft to Optimize Work & Flow" by Dominica DeGrandis

These books offer deeper insights into how categorizing work early on helps streamline processes and lead to better outcomes.

Chapter 2

The Kanban Kerfuffle

Sally stared at her inbox, her eyes glazing over as she scrolled through an endless stream of unread messages. She was about to close her laptop and call it a night when a new email popped up, its subject line blinking like a neon sign: "URGENT: All Hands Meeting Tomorrow - Big Changes Coming!"

"Oh joy," Sally muttered, clicking on the email. "I wonder what fresh hell this is going to be."

As she skimmed the message, her eyebrows shot up. Words like "agile," "lean," and "Kanban" jumped out at her. By the time she finished reading, her head was spinning.

"Kanban?" she said to her cat, Schrödinger, who was lounging on her desk, strategically positioned on top of her most important papers. "Isn't that some kind of Japanese food?"

Schrödinger blinked at her, unimpressed.

"You're right," Sally sighed, reaching for her phone. "I should probably Google this before the meeting."

An hour later, Sally's brain felt like it had been put through a blender. From what she could gather, Kanban was some kind of magical project management system that would solve all their problems. It involved sticky notes, a board, and something called "WIP limits" - which sounded to Sally like a new kind of extreme diet.

"Well," she said to Schrödinger, who had moved to her lap, seeking warmth and attention, "I guess we're about to become Kanban experts. How hard can it be?"

The next morning, Sally arrived at the office early, armed with a grande latte and a vague understanding of Kanban. She found the conference room already buzzing with energy. Their CEO, a man named Frank who always looked like he had just stepped out of a motivational speaker convention, stood at the front of the room, beaming.

"Good morning, team!" Frank boomed as soon as everyone was seated. "Are you ready to revolutionize the way we work?"

A mumble of half-hearted agreement rippled through the room.

"Great enthusiasm!" Frank said, either oblivious to or choosing to ignore the lack of excitement. "As of today, we are implementing Kanban across all our teams!"

He gestured dramatically to a large whiteboard that had been wheeled in. It was divided into three columns: To Do, Doing, and Done.

Frank gestured grandly at the pristine whiteboard, as if unveiling a masterpiece. "Ladies and gentlemen," he declared, his tone dripping with motivational zeal, "behold our Kanban board! A revolutionary tool that will transform how we work."

The room fell silent, save for the faint squeak of a marker cap in Frank's hand. Sally exchanged a wary glance with Dave, whose smirk threatened to break into full-blown laughter. The board's three columns—*To Do, Doing, Done*—stood there, stark and unassuming, like an unfinished sketch of something that was supposed to be groundbreaking.

"Uh, Frank?" Sally ventured. "Isn't Kanban supposed to have more… detail?"

Frank waved her off, his enthusiasm undiminished. "Details are for later! For now, just write down your tasks and slap them on the board. Let's keep those ideas flowing!"

The room erupted into chaos. People scrambled for sticky notes, arguing over which tasks belonged in which column. Sally found herself in a heated debate with Brad from marketing about whether "brainstorm new logo ideas" counted as "Doing" or "To Do."

By the time everyone had placed their tasks on the board, it looked less like an organized system and more like a Jackson Pollock painting made of Post-its.

"Excellent!" Frank exclaimed, apparently delighted by the multicolored mess. "This is Kanban in action, people!"

As Sally stared at the board, she couldn't shake the feeling that they were missing something important. Wasn't there supposed to be some kind of limit on how many tasks could be in progress at once? And shouldn't there be more specific stages than just "Doing"?

But before she could voice her concerns, Frank was ushering everyone out of the room. "Remember," he called after them, "Kanban is all about flexibility and continuous flow. Keep those tasks moving!"

Back at her desk, Sally tried to make sense of her new "Kanban" workflow. She had dutifully written down all her tasks on sticky notes, but now she was faced with a dilemma. Should she start with the task at the top of her "To Do" column? Or the one that was due soonest? Or maybe the one that seemed easiest?

"This is ridiculous," she muttered, reaching for a sticky note at random. "How is this any different from what we were doing before?"

Just as she was about to start on her chosen task - "Update Q3 sales projections" - her phone rang. It was Brad.

"Sally!" he exclaimed before she could even say hello. "I need you to drop everything and work on the new landing page design. It's urgent!"

Sally glanced at her makeshift Kanban board, where "Landing page design" was firmly in the "To Do" column. "But Brad," she started, "according to our new system-"

"Forget the system," Brad interrupted. "This is more important. The client needs it by end of day."

Sighing, Sally moved the "Landing page design" sticky note to her "Doing" column, which was now overflowing with tasks. So much for limiting work in progress.

As the day wore on, Sally found herself constantly shuffling sticky notes back and forth, never seeming to make any real progress. Every time she thought she was close to finishing a task, a new "urgent" request would come in, forcing her to reshuffle her priorities.

By lunchtime, her desk looked like it had been hit by a sticky note tornado. She had long since run out of space on her monitor and had resorted to sticking notes on her coffee mug, her keyboard, and even Schrödinger's cat bed (which she kept under her desk for those long nights at the office).

Desperate for a break, Sally decided to use her lunch hour to grocery shop. "I'll use Kanban to organize my shopping," she thought, feeling a mix of determination and hysteria. "It'll be great practice!"

Armed with a small notebook, Sally created three columns: To Buy, In Cart, and Purchased. She diligently wrote down everything she needed in the "To Buy" column, feeling a small sense of accomplishment.

However, as she wandered the aisles of the supermarket, Sally's Kanban shopping system quickly unraveled. She found herself throwing items into her cart without moving the corresponding sticky notes. When she reached for a can of tuna (Schrödinger's favorite), she realized she had no idea if she had already bought it or not.

"Ma'am," a concerned employee approached her, "are you alright? You've been staring at that can of tuna for five minutes."

Sally looked up, suddenly aware that she had been muttering "To Buy or In Cart?" under her breath. "I'm fine," she said, forcing a smile. "Just... really passionate about tuna."

She left the store with three cans of tuna, no milk, and a vague sense that she had forgotten something important. Her notebook, now covered in hastily scribbled notes and crossed-out items, looked like the work of a conspiracy theorist on a coffee bender.

Back at the office, Sally found her teammates in various states of Kanban-induced confusion. Dave had given up on sticky notes entirely and was now using different colors of string to connect tasks across his monitor, creating what looked like a demented cat's cradle. Tina had disappeared entirely under a mountain of color-coded index cards.

As Sally slumped into her chair, her phone pinged with a calendar reminder: "4 PM - Daily Kanban Standup Meeting."

"Oh god," she groaned, looking at the chaos around her. How was she supposed to give an update when she couldn't even find half her tasks under the sticky note avalanche?

The standup meeting was a disaster. What was supposed to be a quick 15-minute sync turned into a two-hour debate about the definition of "Done." Brad insisted that a task wasn't done until the client had approved it, while Dave argued that it should be considered done as soon as he finished coding it.

"But what about testing?" Tina interjected, waving a handful of bug reports. "We can't call something done if it's full of errors!"

"Testing is a separate task," Dave countered. "It should have its own sticky note!"

As the argument raged on, Sally found herself zoning out, her mind wandering to her failed grocery shopping expedition. She still couldn't shake the feeling that she had forgotten something important.

Finally, mercifully, Frank called an end to the meeting. "Great discussion, team!" he said, seemingly oblivious to the tension in the room. "We'll pick this up again tomorrow. Remember, Kanban is all about continuous improvement!"

As everyone filed out, grumbling and shooting glares at each other, Sally hung back. She approached the Kanban board, now a chaotic mess of overlapping sticky notes in various states of falling off.

"I don't get it," she said to no one in particular. "This was supposed to make things better, wasn't it? So why does it feel like we're even more disorganized than before?"

She plucked a sticky note from the "Done" column. It read "Implement Kanban" in Frank's enthusiastic scrawl.

"Well," Sally sighed, crumpling the note in her hand, "I guess that's one way to define 'Done'."

As she gathered her things to leave, Sally couldn't help but feel a sense of disappointment. She had hoped that Kanban would be the solution to their chaotic workflow, but if anything, it seemed to have made things worse.

On her way out, she passed by Frank's office. He was on the phone, his voice carrying through the partially open door.

"Yes, absolutely!" he was saying. "The Kanban implementation is going great. The team has really taken to it. I think we're ready to start talking about scaling it up to the whole company!"

Sally nearly tripped over her own feet. Scaling up? To the whole company? The thought made her want to curl up under her desk and never come out.

As she drove home, her mind raced with thoughts of sticky notes taking over the entire office, of endless arguments about the definition of "Done," of trying to explain to the CEO why they had delivered precisely zero projects since implementing Kanban.

She pulled into her driveway, still lost in thought, and was halfway to her front door before she realized what she had forgotten at the grocery store.

"Oh, Schrödinger is going to kill me," she muttered, bracing herself for the indignant meows that would greet her.

As she opened her front door, Sally couldn't help but draw a parallel between her forgotten cat food and their botched Kanban implementation. Both were the result of trying to implement a new system without really understanding it, of getting so caught up in the process that you lose sight of the actual goal.

"There has to be a better way," she said to Schrödinger, who was eyeing her suspiciously from his perch on the couch. "Kanban can't really be this... this chaotic, can it?"

Schrödinger, of course, had no answer. He was more concerned with the distinct lack of food in Sally's hands.

As she opened yet another can of tuna for her disgruntled cat, Sally made a decision. Tomorrow, she was going to do some real research on Kanban. There had to be more to it than sticky notes and arguments. And if there wasn't... well, maybe it was time to start looking for a new job.

Little did Sally know, her Kanban journey was just about to unfold. The chaos of today was merely setting the stage for the transformative changes to come. But for now, as she collapsed onto her couch, surrounded by the detritus of her failed Kanban shopping list, all Sally could think was:

Sally stared at the board, a mess of overlapping sticky notes and clashing colors. It reminded her of the time she tried to make a vision board with her niece: hopeful intentions buried under a chaotic pile of glitter and glue. "If this is what order looks like," she muttered under her breath, "maybe chaos wasn't so bad after all."

Manav's Thoughts:

In this chapter, Sally's team rushes into Kanban without fully understanding its principles, leading to chaos. This situation perfectly highlights the need for **Explicit Policies**. Explicit policies outline the rules for moving work items from one stage to another on the Kanban board. They help establish consistency and clarity across the team.

For example, Sally's team could benefit from defining clear criteria for moving a task from "Doing" to "Testing" (e.g., all code is written, peer-reviewed, and passes initial tests). This would reduce misunderstandings and prevent work from moving too early or too late.

From a practical standpoint, explicit policies act as guardrails that help teams maintain quality and avoid confusion. Sally's team, for instance, might establish a policy that no task can move to the next stage until all acceptance criteria are met, preventing incomplete or rushed work from causing delays further down the pipeline.

For further reading on Explicit Policies and their benefits, check out:

- **"Kanban from the Inside" by Mike Burrows**
- **"Actionable Agile Metrics for Predictability" by Daniel S. Vacanti**

Both of these books dive into the mechanics of setting policies and show how they help teams avoid chaos and ensure smooth transitions between workflow stages.

Chapter 3

A Glimmer of Hope

Sally trudged into the office, her shoulders slumped under the weight of yet another chaotic day ahead. The Kanban board loomed in the corner of the room, a technicolor nightmare of overlapping sticky notes and half-erased scribbles. She couldn't help but feel a twinge of resentment towards the innocent-looking whiteboard. After all, it was supposed to be their savior, not another source of stress.

As she settled into her desk, booting up her computer and mentally preparing for the onslaught of emails, a unfamiliar voice caught her attention.

"Well, that's… something," a cheerful voice broke Sally's train of thought. She turned to see a tall man with unruly curls and glasses perched precariously on his nose, studying the board with a mix of amusement and pity.

"'Something,' huh?" Sally said wryly. "I think the word you're looking for is 'disaster.'"

The man grinned. "Chris. New developer. And, uh, let's just say I've seen worse. But not by much."

Sally shook his hand, returning the smile despite her mood. "Sally. Business Analyst and professional chaos wrangler. Welcome aboard… I think."

Chris chuckled. "Thanks. And don't worry, I've seen worse Kanban boards. Though not many," he added with a wink.

Sally's eyebrows shot up. "You've worked with Kanban before?"

"Oh yeah," Chris nodded enthusiastically. "At my last job, we used it for everything. It took a while to get it right, but once we did..." He trailed off, a dreamy look in his eyes. "It was beautiful."

Sally couldn't help but snort. "Beautiful? Our Kanban looks like a toddler's art project gone wrong. How could this possibly be beautiful?"

Chris grinned. Three columns?" Chris asked, pointing to the board. "That's, uh… minimal."

Sally folded her arms. "What's wrong with minimal? It's clean. Simple."

"It's vague," Chris countered with a laugh. "Look, your workflow probably has more stages than this. Right now, it's like a children's map of the world: colorful but missing most of the details."

Sally blinked. It was such a simple observation, but somehow, in all the chaos of their "implementation," no one had thought of it. "I... guess not," she admitted. "But what kind of columns should we add?"

Before Chris could answer, Dave's voice boomed across the office. "Morning standup in five minutes, folks! Don't forget your sticky notes!"

Chris raised an eyebrow. "Sticky notes for standup?"

Sally sighed. "Don't ask. It's Frank's latest 'innovation.' We're supposed to wear our current task as a name tag during the meeting."

As they walked to the conference room, Sally found herself peppering Chris with questions about his previous experiences with Kanban. For the first time since this whole debacle started, she felt a tiny spark of hope. Maybe, just maybe, there was more to this Kanban thing than colorful chaos.

The standup meeting was its usual mess of confusion and conflicting priorities. Sally watched as Chris observed silently, his eyes darting between team members and the overloaded board. When Frank asked if anyone had any questions or suggestions, Chris cleared his throat.

"I hope you don't mind me chiming in on my first day," he began, "but I couldn't help but notice a few things that might help streamline your process."

The room fell silent. Frank beamed, always eager for new ideas (even if he rarely implemented them effectively). "Go ahead, Chris! We're all ears!"

Chris stood up, approaching the board. "Well, first off, have you considered implementing WIP limits?"

The blank stares he received in response were answer enough.

"WIP limits," Chris explained patiently, "are caps on how many items can be in progress at once. It helps prevent overloading and keeps work flowing smoothly."

Sally felt a lightbulb go off in her head. Of course! That's what had been nagging at her all this time. They had been so focused on moving tasks across the board that they'd completely ignored the concept of limiting work in progress.

As Chris continued to explain, touching on concepts like pull systems and cycle time, Sally found herself hanging on every word. It was like he was speaking a language she'd been trying to learn, filling in the gaps that had been driving her crazy.

After the meeting, Sally cornered Chris by the coffee machine. "Okay, spill," she demanded. "Where did you learn all this? And why does it sound so different from what we've been doing?"

Chris laughed. "Well, I had a great mentor at my last job. Guy named Mike. He's kind of a Kanban guru. Taught me everything I know."

Sally's eyes lit up. "A Kanban guru? Do you think... I mean, would he be willing to talk to me? Us? Our team?"

Chris considered for a moment. "I can certainly ask him. He loves talking about Kanban almost as much as he loves implementing it. I'm sure he'd be happy to chat."

As Chris pulled out his phone to send a quick text, Sally felt a wave of excitement wash over her. This could be it – the key to unlocking the true potential of Kanban and finally bringing some order to their chaos.

The rest of the day passed in a blur. Sally found herself looking at their processes with new eyes, mentally noting all the places where Chris's suggestions could make a difference. She even caught herself doodling potential new column layouts for their board during a particularly boring meeting with Brad from marketing.

As she packed up to leave, Chris popped by her desk. "Good news," he grinned. "Mike's happy to meet with us. How does next week sound?"

Sally couldn't contain her enthusiasm. "Next week sounds perfect! Thank you, Chris. Really."

On her way home, Sally's mind was buzzing with possibilities. She barely noticed the usual traffic snarl-up, her thoughts occupied with WIP limits and workflow optimization. It wasn't until she pulled into her driveway that she realized she'd forgotten to stop at the grocery store. Again.

Sighing, she trudged into the house, bracing herself for Schrödinger's judgmental meows. But as she opened the door, an idea struck her.

"Kanban grocery list," she muttered, hurrying to her home office. She grabbed a small whiteboard and some markers, quickly sketching out columns: "To Buy," "Low," "Stocked."

It wasn't perfect, but as she filled it out, moving items between columns based on what she knew was in her pantry, she felt a sense of control she hadn't experienced in weeks.

Stepping back, she admired her handiwork. It was simple, yes, but somehow it made the daunting task of keeping her kitchen stocked seem manageable.

"Well, Schrödinger," she said to the cat who had wandered in to investigate, "looks like we might be onto something here."

Schrödinger meowed, either in approval of the new system or in reminder that his food bowl was still empty.

As Sally opened a can of tuna (mental note: move "Cat Food" to "To Buy" column immediately), she couldn't help but feel a surge of optimism. If this small change could make such a difference in her personal life, imagine what proper Kanban could do for their team at work.

She fell asleep that night with visions of smoothly flowing tasks and perfectly balanced workflows dancing in her head. For the first time in weeks, she felt genuinely excited about going to work the next day.

Little did Sally know, her Kanban journey was about to kick into high gear. The meeting with Mike loomed on the horizon, promising to be the catalyst that would transform not just their work processes, but Sally's entire approach to managing the chaos of daily life.

As she drifted off to sleep, a small smile played on her lips. Tomorrow was a new day, and with it came the promise of a whole new way of working. Sally couldn't wait to see where this Kanban adventure would take her next.

Manav's Thoughts:

As Chris points out the flaws in the team's current approach, it's a great time to introduce **Service Level Expectations (SLEs)**. SLEs help manage expectations around how long a task might take to complete, based on historical performance data. For Sally's team, SLEs would provide clarity for both the team and stakeholders, offering a more predictable workflow.

By setting expectations around how long different types of tasks typically take (e.g., "bug fixes are completed within 3 days"), the team can improve trust with stakeholders and reduce last-minute pressure. SLEs also help the team know when work is overdue and whether something needs to be expedited or deprioritized.

In practical terms, implementing SLEs enables teams to focus on predictability rather than meeting arbitrary deadlines. Over time, this leads to better work planning and stakeholder satisfaction.

For further reading on SLEs and how to apply them, consider:

- "Kanban Maturity Model" by David J. Anderson & Teodora Bozheva
- "The Principles of Product Development Flow: Second Generation Lean Product Development" by Donald G. Reinertsen

These resources provide actionable insights into SLEs and how to manage customer expectations effectively through Kanban.

Chapter 4

Kanban 101: Seeing the Work

Sally arrived at the office an hour early, armed with a triple-shot espresso and a determination that bordered on desperation. Today was the day she'd meet Mike, the fabled Kanban guru, and she was not about to let this opportunity slip through her fingers like so many half-baked productivity schemes before.

As she approached the conference room, she heard voices. Peering inside, she saw Chris chatting animatedly with a man she assumed must be Mike. He was older than she expected, with salt-and-pepper hair and laugh lines etched deep around his eyes. He looked less like a productivity expert and more like someone's favorite uncle who told great stories at family barbecues.

"Ah, you must be Sally!" Mike's voice boomed as he caught sight of her hovering in the doorway. "Come in, come in! We were just about to start the fun!"

Sally couldn't help but raise an eyebrow. "Fun? I didn't realize Kanban and fun were allowed in the same sentence."

Mike's laugh filled the room. "Oh, you'd be surprised. Now, let's start with a little exercise. I want you to close your eyes and picture your current workflow. Don't think too hard, just let the image come to you naturally."

Sally obliged, squeezing her eyes shut. Almost immediately, her mind conjured up an image of a tornado filled with sticky notes, coffee cups, and screaming colleagues. She felt her cheeks flush with embarrassment.

"Okay, now open your eyes and tell me what you saw," Mike prompted.

Sally hesitated. "Um... chaos? Like a whirlwind of tasks and deadlines all mixed up together."

Mike nodded sagely. "That's a common visualization. Now, let's see if we can bring some order to that chaos, shall we?"

He turned to the whiteboard that covered one wall of the conference room and uncapped a marker. "Let's start at the beginning. What's the very first thing that happens when a new piece of work comes in?"

Sally thought for a moment. "Well, usually it starts with a request from a client or stakeholder..."

"Excellent!" Mike drew a box on the left side of the board and labeled it 'Incoming Requests.' "Now, what happens next?"

As Sally described each step of their process, Mike added boxes and arrows to the board. Slowly but surely, a map of their workflow began to take shape. It wasn't the neat, linear process Sally had always imagined, but rather a complex web of interconnected steps, decision points, and feedback loops.

"Now," Mike said, stepping back from the board, "take a look at this and tell me what you see."

Sally stared at the diagram, her eyes widening as realization dawned. "I... I had no idea we had so many steps. And look at all these places where work gets stuck or sent back!"

Mike nodded encouragingly. "That's right. This is your real workflow, warts and all. Now, let's identify where your main bottlenecks are."

As they discussed each step, Sally felt like scales were falling from her eyes. She saw how work piled up in certain areas, how some tasks bounced back and forth between teams, and how some crucial steps were often overlooked or rushed.

"Oh my god," she murmured, "no wonder we're always putting out fires. We never even knew where to look for the smoke!"

Chris, who had been quietly observing, chimed in. "It's pretty eye-opening, isn't it? I remember having the same reaction when Mike first did this exercise with my old team."

Mike smiled. "The power of visualization is often underestimated. Now, let's take this a step further. Sally, I want you to think about your personal life. Is there any area where you feel particularly disorganized or overwhelmed?"

Sally didn't have to think long. "My vacation planning. I've been trying to organize a trip to Europe for months, but it always feels like there's too much to do and not enough time."

"Perfect!" Mike exclaimed. "Let's map that out too."

Over the next half hour, they created a visual representation of Sally's vacation planning process. Just like with her work workflow, hidden complexities and bottlenecks emerged.

"Wait a minute," Sally muttered, staring at the web of sticky notes representing her vacation planning. "I've been jumping straight to booking flights without even deciding on dates first? That's like trying to frost a cake before baking it."

Mike chuckled. "Exactly. And just like baking, planning has a sequence. Skip steps, and you'll end up with a mess—or worse, no cake at all."

Sally laughed, a weight lifting from her shoulders. "So what you're saying is... my chaos isn't special, just badly structured?"

"Precisely!" Mike said with a wink.

As the meeting wound down, Sally felt a mixture of excitement and slight overwhelm. "This is amazing," she said, "but how do we translate this into our daily work? Our current board is... well, let's just say it's more decorative than functional."

Mike chuckled. "That's where the real fun begins. Tomorrow, we'll take this workflow and turn it into a proper Kanban board. But for now, I want you to go back to your team and share what you've learned. Start getting them excited about the possibilities."

Sally left the conference room with her head spinning, but in a good way. For the first time in months, she felt like she had a clear picture of what needed to be done.

That evening, as she sat at her kitchen table surrounded by travel brochures and her laptop, Sally found herself reaching for a blank sheet of paper. Without really thinking about it, she began to sketch out a simplified version of the vacation planning workflow Mike had helped her create.

As she added sticky notes for each task, moving them through the process, she felt a sense of calm settle over her. The trip that had seemed so daunting now felt manageable, broken down into clear, actionable steps.

"Well, Schrödinger," she said to her cat, who was eyeing the colorful sticky notes with feline disdain, "looks like we might actually make it to Paris this year. What do you think about that?"

Schrödinger's only response was to bat a fallen sticky note off the table, but Sally chose to interpret it as enthusiastic approval.

The next morning, Sally practically bounced into the office. She'd spent half the night dreaming about perfectly organized workflows and smoothly flowing tasks. As she approached the team's workspace, she saw Chris already there, erasing their old, chaotic board.

"Ready to revolutionize our workflow?" he asked with a grin.

Sally rolled up her sleeves. "Let's do this."

Over the next few hours, with guidance from Mike via video call, they transformed their Kanban board. Gone were the vague "To Do," "Doing," and "Done" columns. In their place, a series of clearly defined steps emerged, each representing a crucial part of their process.

As team members trickled in, their reactions ranged from curiosity to skepticism to outright confusion.

"What happened to our board?" Dave asked, coffee mug frozen halfway to his lips.

"We've had a Kanban makeover," Sally explained, unable to keep the excitement from her voice. "Come on, I'll show you how it works."

As she walked her teammates through the new board, Sally could see the light of understanding dawning in their eyes. Tina from QA actually clapped when she saw the dedicated "Testing" column.

"You mean I won't have to hunt people down to find out what needs testing anymore?" she asked, her voice filled with wonder.

"That's right," Sally confirmed. "And look, we've set WIP limits for each column. That means we won't be overloading any one part of our process."

By lunchtime, the entire team was buzzing with excitement. Even Frank, initially skeptical of changing his "perfectly good system," had to admit that the new board made a lot more sense.

As Sally stepped back to admire their handiwork, she felt a sense of pride and accomplishment wash over her. The board wasn't just a collection of tasks anymore; it was a clear, visual representation of their entire workflow. For the first time in months, she felt like they had a handle on their work.

"Not bad for a day's work, huh?" Chris said, coming to stand beside her.

Sally nodded, a smile playing on her lips. "Not bad at all. But something tells me we're just getting started."

As if on cue, her phone buzzed with a message from Mike: "Great job on the board! Ready to learn about stand-ups and flow metrics tomorrow?"

Sally's grin widened. She had a feeling that this Kanban journey was about to get even more interesting. And for once, she couldn't wait to see what challenges tomorrow would bring.

Manav's Thoughts:

Now that Sally's team is visualizing their work properly on the Kanban board, it's time to introduce **Classes of Service**. Classes of Service are used to categorize work based on its urgency or risk and apply different rules for how that work is managed.

For example, Sally's team could introduce an "Expedite" lane for critical bugs that need to be fixed immediately and limit the number of tasks in that lane to prevent overloading. Meanwhile, other lanes might have more relaxed WIP limits to allow for ongoing development.

From a practical standpoint, Classes of Service help teams prioritize work based on the context of the task, ensuring that urgent items are dealt with swiftly while other tasks continue to flow through the system. It also helps to align work with business priorities, ensuring that high-value work is not delayed by less important tasks.

To learn more about Classes of Service and how to implement them, consider reading:

- "Essential Kanban Condensed" by David J. Anderson & Andy Carmichael
- "Personal Kanban: Mapping Work | Navigating Life" by Jim Benson & Tonianne DeMaria Barry

Both books explain how to balance different types of work using Classes of Service, making sure high-priority work doesn't disrupt the flow of the overall system.

Chapter 5

Stop Starting, Start Finishing

Sally stared at the new Kanban board, a mixture of pride and trepidation swirling in her stomach. The neat columns and carefully arranged sticky notes were a far cry from the chaotic mess they'd been dealing with just days ago. But as she watched her teammates excitedly adding more and more tasks to the board, a niggling worry began to form in the back of her mind.

"Looks great, doesn't it?" Chris's voice startled her out of her reverie.

"It does," Sally agreed, then hesitated. "But... don't you think we might be getting a bit carried away?"

Chris followed her gaze to the 'In Progress' column, which was rapidly filling up with colorful sticky notes. "Ah," he said, a knowing smile playing on his lips. "I think it's time we talked about WIP limits."

"Whip what now?" Sally asked, raising an eyebrow.

"WIP. Work In Progress," Chris explained. "It's one of the key principles of Kanban. Remember how Mike mentioned it yesterday?"

Sally nodded slowly, the memory surfacing. "Right, the caps on how many items can be in progress at once. But how do we actually implement that?"

Chris grinned. "I thought you'd never ask. Hey, team!" he called out, raising his voice to be heard over the buzz of activity. "Gather 'round. It's time for a little Kanban magic!"

As the team assembled, looking equal parts curious and skeptical, Chris began to explain the concept of WIP limits. Sally found herself drawn in, nodding along as Chris described how limiting work in progress could lead to better focus, faster completion times, and higher quality work.

"Imagine you're juggling," Chris began, picking up a few nearby pens for emphasis. "One, two, maybe three balls—manageable, right?" He added a fourth pen, then a fifth, and promptly fumbled, sending pens clattering to the floor.

"Add too much, and you drop everything," he said, retrieving the pens with a sheepish grin. "That's what happens when we overload our workflow. WIP limits let us focus on what we can actually finish."

Dave, the lead developer, snorted. "That's all well and good, but we've got deadlines to meet. We can't just stop working on things because of some arbitrary limit."

Chris smiled patiently. "Actually, Dave, that's exactly what we're going to do. But don't worry, it's not as scary as it sounds. In fact, I bet we'll meet those deadlines faster than ever."

He turned to the board and began drawing boxes around each column. "These," he explained, "are our WIP limits. We're going to calculate the right number for each column based on our team's capacity."

What followed was a flurry of activity as the team worked together to determine their limits. Sally found herself caught up in the excitement, helping to crunch numbers and debate the merits of different limits for each stage of their process.

"Okay," Chris said finally, stepping back from the board. "Let's give these a try. Remember, once a column hits its limit, no new work can be added until something moves out."

The team nodded, a mix of determination and uncertainty on their faces. As they dispersed to begin their day, Sally couldn't help but wonder how this would play out in practice.

She didn't have to wait long to find out.

Barely an hour into the morning, Brad from marketing burst into the office, his face flushed with excitement. "Gang, I've got great news! The CEO loved our pitch for the new product line. He wants us to start working on it right away!"

A chorus of groans met this announcement. Sally glanced at the Kanban board, where every column was already at its WIP limit.

"Um, Brad," she began hesitantly, "that's great news, but we're kind of at capacity right now."

Brad's face fell. "What do you mean, 'at capacity'? This is a priority project! We need to start on it immediately!"

Sally took a deep breath, steeling herself. "I understand, but look at our board. We've implemented WIP limits to help us focus and be more productive. If we start on this new project now, we'll have to stop work on something else."

Brad's eyes narrowed. "WIP limits? Is this another one of Frank's crazy ideas?"

"Actually," Chris interjected smoothly, "it's a core principle of Kanban. By limiting our work in progress, we can finish tasks faster and deliver more value to our customers."

Brad looked unconvinced. "But this is important! Surely we can make an exception?"

Sally felt a moment of panic. It would be so easy to give in, to say yes and cram one more thing onto their already full plate. But then she remembered Mike's words about the importance of respecting WIP limits.

"I'm sorry, Brad," she said, surprised by the firmness in her voice. "We can't start on this right away. But," she added quickly, seeing the storm clouds gathering on Brad's face, "we can prioritize it for the next available slot. In fact, because we're focusing on finishing our current work, that slot will probably open up sooner than you think."

Brad huffed and puffed for a few more minutes, but eventually left, muttering about "newfangled management techniques." As the door closed behind him, Sally let out a breath she didn't realize she'd been holding.

"Nice job," Chris said quietly, giving her a thumbs up.

As the day wore on, Sally was surprised to find that the WIP limits, far from slowing them down, seemed to be having a positive effect. Without the constant context-switching that came from juggling too many tasks, team members were able to focus deeply on their work. Tasks that had been languishing for days were suddenly getting finished.

By the end of the day, they had completed more work than they typically did in two or three days. The sense of accomplishment was palpable, with team members high-fiving each other as they moved sticky notes to the 'Done' column.

As Sally packed up to leave, she felt a sense of excitement she hadn't experienced at work in months. She was eager to see how this new way of working would continue to evolve.

On her way home, she stopped at the gym, determined to keep up with her fitness routine despite the long day. As she changed into her workout clothes, she found herself thinking about WIP limits.

"I wonder..." she mused aloud, earning a strange look from a woman at the next locker.

Instead of her usual haphazard approach of bouncing between different machines and exercises, Sally decided to apply the principle of WIP limits to her workout. She focused on completing one full set of exercises before moving on to the next, resisting the urge to switch tasks when things got tough.

To her surprise, she finished her workout faster than usual, and with a greater sense of accomplishment. As she cooled down on the treadmill, she couldn't help but chuckle at how Kanban was seeping into every aspect of her life.

Back at home, sweaty but invigorated, Sally decided to tackle another area of her life that often felt overwhelming: meal prep. Usually, she'd try to cook multiple dishes at once, resulting in a kitchen that looked like a disaster zone and meals that were often half-burned or undercooked.

This time, she applied the WIP limit principle. She focused on preparing one dish at a time, moving through her recipes with a methodical focus that felt almost meditative. To her delight, not only did she finish cooking faster, but everything turned out perfectly cooked.

As she sat down to enjoy her meal, Schrödinger curled up at her feet, she reflected on the day's events. The challenges of implementing WIP limits at work, the satisfaction of standing firm against Brad's demands, the surprising benefits she'd discovered in her personal life – it all swirled together in her mind.

She realized that this Kanban journey was about more than just improving work processes. It was about changing how she approached life itself. The idea both thrilled and terrified her.

The next morning, Sally arrived at the office early, eager to see how the team would handle their second day with WIP limits. To her surprise, she found Dave already there, intently studying the Kanban board.

"Morning, Dave," she said cautiously, unsure of what to expect. Dave had been one of the most vocal skeptics of the WIP limits yesterday.

To her shock, Dave turned to her with a broad smile. "Sally! You're not going to believe this. I stayed late last night to finish up that tricky bug I've been wrestling with for days. Without any other tasks competing for my attention, I finally cracked it!"

Sally felt a surge of excitement. "That's fantastic, Dave! How do you feel about the WIP limits now?"

Dave shook his head ruefully. "I hate to admit it, but I think I'm becoming a convert. It's like... for the first time in months, I can actually hear myself think."

As the rest of the team trickled in, similar stories emerged. Tina from QA reported that she'd cleared her entire backlog of tests. Alex, the UX designer, proudly showed off three completed design mockups that had been languishing half-finished for weeks.

Even Brad from marketing stopped by, looking slightly sheepish. "So, uh, about that new project," he began.

Sally braced herself for another argument, but Brad surprised her. "I talked to the CEO, explained the whole WIP limit thing. He was skeptical at first, but when I showed him how much progress you guys made yesterday... well, let's just say he's intrigued. He wants a full presentation on this Kanban stuff next week."

Sally's jaw dropped. "Really? That's... wow, that's great, Brad! Thank you!"

As Brad left, Chris sidled up to Sally. "Looks like our little Kanban experiment is starting to make some waves," he said with a grin.

Sally nodded, still processing the morning's events. "I can't believe how quickly things are changing. It's like... like we've suddenly unlocked a superpower we didn't know we had."

Chris laughed. "That's one way to put it. But remember, we're just getting started. We've still got a lot to learn about Kanban."

"Bring it on," Sally said, surprising herself with her enthusiasm. "I can't wait to see what's next."

As if on cue, her phone buzzed with a message from Mike: "Heard about your WIP limit success. Ready to talk about pull systems and flow efficiency tomorrow?"

Sally grinned, already anticipating the new challenges and insights that lay ahead. For the first time in her career, she felt like she was part of something truly transformative. The chaos that had defined her work life for so long was giving way to a sense of flow and purpose.

As she turned back to the Kanban board, ready to start another productive day, Sally couldn't help but feel a sense of excitement about the future. The journey from chaos to flow was well underway, and she was leading the charge.

Little did she know, the biggest challenges – and the most profound changes – were yet to come. But for now, Sally was content to bask in the glow of their first real victory. They had stopped starting and started finishing, and the results spoke for themselves.

The Kanban revolution had begun, and there was no turning back now.

Manav's Thoughts:

The introduction of WIP limits is one of the most powerful aspects of Kanban. However, one of the most common challenges teams face after setting WIP limits is dealing with **Blockers**—tasks that are stuck due to dependencies or other issues. Managing blockers is crucial to maintaining flow and ensuring that work progresses smoothly through the system.

Sally's team could benefit from introducing **Blocker Clustering**—a method that groups similar types of blockers together to identify patterns. For example, if tasks frequently get blocked because they're waiting for external approval, that points to a process issue that needs to be addressed.

From a practical standpoint, addressing blockers as clusters allows teams to solve systemic issues rather than treating each blocked task as an isolated incident. Sally's team could create a visual representation of blockers on the board (e.g., using red stickers) and track how often and why tasks get blocked.

For more on managing blockers and improving flow, I recommend:

- "The Phoenix Project: A Novel about IT, DevOps, and Helping Your Business Win" by Gene Kim, Kevin Behr, and George Spafford
- "The Goal: A Process of Ongoing Improvement" by Eliyahu M. Goldratt

These books provide a narrative approach to dealing with blockers and constraints in workflows, making them relatable and actionable.

Chapter 6

Pull, Don't Push

Sally stood in front of the Kanban board, sipping her morning coffee and admiring the neat columns of sticky notes. The team had been using WIP limits for a week now, and the difference was noticeable. Tasks were moving across the board more smoothly, and there was a palpable sense of accomplishment in the air.

But something still wasn't quite right. Sally couldn't put her finger on it, but there was a nagging feeling that they were missing a crucial piece of the Kanban puzzle.

As if summoned by her thoughts, Chris appeared at her elbow. "Morning, Sally. Contemplating the mysteries of the universe?"

Sally chuckled. "More like the mysteries of Kanban. I feel like we're on the right track, but something's still off."

Chris nodded sagely. "Ah, I think I know what you mean. Tell me, how do tasks usually end up on our board?"

Sally furrowed her brow. "Well, we have our backlog, and then we assign tasks to team members based on priority and their expertise."

"Exactly," Chris said. "We're pushing work onto people. But what if we tried a different approach?"

Before Sally could ask what he meant, the office door burst open and in strode Frank, their ever-enthusiastic CEO, followed by a harried-looking Brad from marketing.

"Good morning, team!" Frank boomed. "I hope you're all ready for an exciting day. We've got a new urgent project that needs immediate attention!"

Sally felt her stomach drop. They'd just gotten into a good rhythm with their WIP limits, and now this? She glanced at Chris, who gave her a reassuring nod.

"Frank, Brad," Sally greeted, plastering on her best polite-but-weary smile. "You both look energized. Dare I ask what fresh disaster—sorry, opportunity—has landed on our plates today?"

Frank's grin didn't waver. "It's not a disaster, Sally. It's an *opportunity*."

Brad leaned in, already buzzing with excitement. "Big client, big stakes. They need updates to the website, like, yesterday."

Sally bit back a groan. "And here I thought we were aiming for flow, not fire drills."

Chris cleared his throat. "Frank, Brad, this sounds like an exciting opportunity. But before we dive in, I'd like to introduce you to a concept that might help us handle this more effectively."

Frank paused mid-sentence, looking intrigued. "Go on, Chris. I'm all ears."

Chris smiled. "It's called a pull system. Instead of pushing new work onto the team, we let them pull work when they have the capacity to handle it."

Brad looked skeptical. "But this is urgent. We can't just wait around for someone to decide they're ready to work on it."

"Actually," Chris said, "a pull system can help us handle urgent work more efficiently. Let me show you how."

Over the next hour, Chris explained the basics of a pull system to the team, Frank, and Brad. Sally found herself nodding along, the pieces finally falling into place.

"So, instead of assigning tasks," Sally summarized, "we'll have a prioritized backlog, and team members will pull the next highest priority task when they're ready for new work?"

"Exactly," Chris beamed. "It puts the control in the hands of the people doing the work, which leads to better flow and less stress."

Frank looked thoughtful. "I like the sound of that. But how do we handle truly urgent tasks?"

Chris walked over to the Kanban board and drew a new column labeled "Expedite." "We can have a special lane for urgent work. But here's the key — we limit it to one item at a time. That way, we can handle urgent tasks without completely disrupting our workflow."

As the team discussed the new system, Sally could see the mixture of excitement and apprehension on their faces. Change was never easy, but this felt like a step in the right direction.

"Alright," Frank said finally. "Let's give it a try. Brad, work with the team to get your urgent project into the expedite lane. But remember, only one item at a time!"

As Frank and Brad left, the team gathered around the board.

"So, who wants to pull the first task?" Chris asked.

There was a moment of hesitation before Dave, their lead developer, stepped forward. "I'll give it a shot," he said, reaching for a sticky note from the backlog.

Over the next few days, Sally watched in amazement as the team adapted to the pull system. There were hiccups, of course. Old habits died hard, and she often caught herself wanting to assign tasks to people.

"Remember, Sally," Chris would gently remind her, "pull, don't push."

The real test came a week into the new system when Brad burst into the office, his face flushed with panic. "We need to make changes to the website ASAP! The client just called with new requirements!"

In the past, this would have thrown the entire team into chaos. But now, Sally calmly walked Brad over to the Kanban board.

"Let's take a look at our current work and see where we can fit this in," she said, surprising herself with her composure.

They moved Brad's task into the Expedite lane, and Dave, who had just finished his current task, pulled it immediately. The rest of the team continued their work uninterrupted.

Brad watched in astonishment. "That's it? No shuffling everything around? No all-hands-on-deck panic?"

Sally smiled. "Welcome to the world of pull systems, Brad. Less stress, more flow."

As Brad left, visibly relieved, Sally couldn't help but feel a sense of pride. They were really starting to get the hang of this Kanban thing.

Inspired by the changes at work, Sally decided to apply the pull system to her personal life. Her first target? Her daily commute.

Usually, Sally would rush to catch the earliest possible bus, stressing herself out in the process. But today, she decided to try something different. She got ready at a leisurely pace and arrived at the bus stop just in time for her usual bus.

To her surprise, the bus was less crowded than usual, and she even managed to snag a seat. As she settled in for the ride, she realized she felt calmer and more prepared for the day ahead.

"Pull, don't push," she murmured to herself, earning a curious glance from the passenger next to her.

Back at the office, Sally noticed a change in the team's dynamic. People seemed more relaxed, yet paradoxically more productive. Tasks were flowing smoothly across the board, and there was less of the frantic energy that used to permeate the office.

During their daily standup, Tina from QA spoke up. "I never thought I'd say this, but I actually look forward to pulling new tasks now. It feels... I don't know, empowering?"

Dave nodded in agreement. "Yeah, and I'm not constantly context-switching anymore. I can focus on one thing at a time, knowing that when I'm done, there's always a clear next step."

As the days went by, Sally found herself applying the pull system to more areas of her life. Grocery shopping became a breeze as she pulled items from her list based on what aisle she was in, rather than crisscrossing the store in a haphazard fashion.

Even her Netflix queue benefited from the pull system. Instead of endlessly scrolling and pushing herself to watch the latest buzzworthy show, she created a prioritized list and pulled from it when she was in the mood for TV.

One evening, as she settled onto her couch with a bowl of popcorn and Schrödinger curled up beside her, Sally reflected on how much had changed in just a few short weeks.

"You know, Schrödinger," she said, scratching behind the cat's ears, "I think we might be onto something here."

Schrödinger purred in response, clearly more interested in the popcorn than Kanban principles.

The next day at work, Sally arrived to find Chris already at the Kanban board, making some adjustments.

"Morning, Chris. What's new in the world of Kanban today?"

Chris grinned. "Oh, just a little something I like to call 'flow efficiency.' Want to learn about it?"

Sally felt a mixture of excitement and trepidation. Every time Chris introduced a new concept, it led to both breakthroughs and challenges. But she couldn't deny the positive impact Kanban was having on their team.

"Alright," she said, setting down her coffee mug. "Hit me with your flow efficiency wisdom."

As Chris began explaining, Sally found herself drawn in once again. She realized that this journey into Kanban was far from over. In fact, it felt like they were just scratching the surface.

But for now, as she looked at their Kanban board with its smoothly flowing tasks and relaxed, focused team members, Sally knew they were on the right track. They had learned to pull, not push, and the results spoke for themselves.

As the team gathered for their morning standup, there was a palpable sense of anticipation in the air. They had come so far, but Sally knew that the real challenges – and the real rewards – were still to come.

"Alright, team," she said, clapping her hands together. "Who's ready to pull some tasks and make some magic happen?"

The enthusiastic response from her teammates told her all she needed to know. They were ready for whatever Kanban had in store for them next. The journey from chaos to flow was well underway, and there was no turning back now.

Little did Sally know, the lessons in flow efficiency that Chris was about to share would take their Kanban practice to a whole new level. But that, as they say, is a story for another chapter.

Manav's Thoughts:

As Sally's team moves to a pull-based system, they're learning to control the flow of work more effectively. One advanced concept that could enhance their process is **Flow Efficiency**—a metric that measures the ratio of time work is actively being worked on versus the time it spends waiting in queues.

In Sally's case, improving flow efficiency could help them identify where work is waiting too long between stages. For example, a task might be waiting for testing for several days, even though it only takes a few hours to complete once it's being actively worked on.

Improving flow efficiency involves reducing waiting times and ensuring that tasks move smoothly from one stage to the next. This leads to faster delivery times and improved productivity without the need to increase effort or resources.

To learn more about Flow Efficiency and how to measure it, check out:

- **"Lean Thinking: Banish Waste and Create Wealth in Your Corporation" by James P. Womack and Daniel T. Jones**
- **"Lean Product and Process Development" by Allen C. Ward**

These books explore how reducing waste and improving flow efficiency lead to more streamlined and productive teams.

Chapter 7

Smooth Operator: Optimizing Flow

Sally stared at the Kanban board, her brow furrowed in concentration. Something wasn't quite right, but she couldn't put her finger on it. The team had been using their pull system for a few weeks now, and while things had definitely improved, there was still a nagging sense that they could do better.

"Sally," Chris's voice cut through her thoughts like a splash of cold water. "You've been staring at that board for ten minutes. I'm starting to worry you've entered a Kanban-induced trance."

She blinked, startled. "Sorry. Just... thinking. The board looks better, but I can't shake the feeling we're missing something."

Chris stepped closer, his eyes scanning the columns. "Missing? Or maybe... clogged? Let's check for bottlenecks."

Before Sally could respond, a commotion at the other end of the office caught their attention. Tina from QA was engaged in what looked like an intense game of charades with Dave, the lead developer.

"No, no, no!" Tina was saying, waving her arms frantically. "I can't start testing until you fix the login bug. It's blocking everything!"

Dave ran a hand through his hair, frustration evident on his face. "But I can't fix the login bug until I finish the payment gateway integration. It's all connected!"

Sally and Chris exchanged knowing glances. "Houston, we have a bottleneck," Chris murmured.

As they approached the feuding pair, Sally couldn't help but draw a parallel to her recent vacation planning experience. She'd spent hours meticulously organizing their itinerary, only to have the entire trip derailed by an unexpected delay at airport security. One slow checkpoint had backed up the entire system, causing a ripple effect of missed connections and frayed nerves.

"Guys," Sally interjected, stepping between Tina and Dave. "I think we need to take a step back and look at the bigger picture here. Chris, didn't you mention something about flow metrics earlier?"

Chris nodded enthusiastically. "Indeed I did. Let's gather the team and do a little flow analysis, shall we?"

As the team assembled around the Kanban board, Chris began explaining the concept of flow metrics. "We're going to look at three key measurements: lead time, cycle time, and throughput," he said, scribbling the terms on a nearby whiteboard.

"Lead time," he continued, "is the total time it takes for a task to go from 'requested' to 'done'. Cycle time is how long it spends in our active workflow. And throughput is simply how many items we complete in a given time period."

Sally nodded along, her mind already racing with possibilities. "So if we track these metrics, we can identify where work is getting stuck and why?"

"Exactly!" Chris beamed. "Let's set up a simple spreadsheet to start tracking this data."

Over the next hour, the team huddled around Sally's computer, setting up a basic tracking system for their flow metrics. As they input data from the past few weeks, patterns began to emerge.

"Look at this," Sally pointed out, highlighting a column on the spreadsheet. "Our cycle time spikes dramatically when tasks hit the testing phase. That's our bottleneck!"

Tina shifted uncomfortably. "It's not that I'm slow," she defended. "It's just that by the time tasks get to me, they're often blocked by bugs or incomplete features."

Dave nodded in agreement. "And sometimes I'm already knee-deep in the next task before I hear about issues in testing. Context switching is killing our productivity."

As the team discussed potential solutions, Sally's mind wandered to her attempts at optimizing her home cooking routine. She'd tried to channel her inner chef, timing multiple dishes to be ready simultaneously. The result? A kitchen that looked like a tornado had hit it, and a meal where the pasta was cold, the sauce was burnt, and the garlic bread was forgotten entirely in the oven.

Snapping back to the present, Sally had an idea. "What if we tried pairing developers and testers earlier in the process? Instead of throwing completed work 'over the wall' to testing, we could collaborate from the start."

The team mulled this over, and gradually, a new workflow began to take shape. Developers and testers would work together from the beginning of each task, writing tests alongside the code and addressing issues as they arose.

"This could also help with our WIP limits," Chris pointed out. "By combining development and testing efforts, we're essentially creating a single 'in progress' stage for each task."

As they implemented this new approach, Sally couldn't help but see parallels in her daily life. She thought about her commute, where she'd often try to squeeze in multiple errands, jumping off the bus at different stops. More often than not, this led to missed connections and a frantic rush to get everything done.

Inspired by the team's new workflow, Sally decided to apply the same principle to her errands. Instead of trying to do everything at once, she focused on one task per trip, ensuring it was completed fully before moving on to the next. To her surprise, this actually saved time in the long run, as she wasn't constantly backtracking or dealing with half-finished tasks.

Back at the office, the effects of the new workflow were quickly becoming apparent. The Kanban board showed a smoother flow of tasks, with fewer items getting stuck in the testing phase. Tina and Dave, once at odds, were now working side by side, tackling issues as they arose.

"You know," Dave said during one of their daily stand-ups, "I never realized how much time we were wasting with back-and-forth on bugs. This new way of working feels so much more... I don't know, streamlined?"

Tina nodded in agreement. "And I feel like I have a much better understanding of the features before they even reach formal testing. It's like we've eliminated a whole layer of confusion."

As the weeks went by, Sally continued to refine their flow metrics tracking. She added visualizations like cumulative flow diagrams, which helped the team identify trends and potential issues before they became major bottlenecks.

One morning, as Sally was updating their metrics, she noticed something remarkable. "Hey team," she called out, unable to keep the excitement from her voice. "Check this out!"

The team gathered around her desk, peering at the screen.

"Our lead time has decreased by 30% since we implemented the new workflow," Sally explained, pointing to a graph. "And look at our throughput – we're completing 20% more tasks per week!"

A cheer went up from the team. Even Frank, who had been skeptically watching their Kanban experiment from afar, looked impressed.

"Well done, team," he said, a rare smile crossing his face. "I have to admit, I was skeptical about all this Kanban business, but these results speak for themselves."

As the excitement died down and the team returned to their tasks, Sally found herself reflecting on their journey so far. They'd come so far from the chaotic, overwhelmed group they'd been just a few months ago. Now, they moved with purpose, each task flowing smoothly from one stage to the next.

That evening, as Sally prepared dinner in her kitchen, she found herself applying the principles of flow without even thinking about it. She prepped ingredients in advance, cleaned as she went, and focused on one dish at a time. The result? A perfectly timed meal and a kitchen that didn't look like a disaster zone.

As she sat down to enjoy her dinner, Schrödinger curled up at her feet, Sally couldn't help but marvel at how much Kanban had changed her life, both at work and at home. The chaos that had once defined her days had given way to a sense of purposeful flow.

Her phone buzzed with a message from Chris: "Great job with the flow metrics! Ready to tackle cumulative flow diagrams tomorrow?"

Sally grinned, already anticipating the new challenges and insights that lay ahead. She typed back a quick reply: "Bring it on! I've got a feeling we're just getting started."

As she hit send, Sally realized that this Kanban journey was far from over. In fact, it felt like they were just starting to scratch the surface of what was possible. But one thing was certain – they were no longer drowning in chaos. They were surfing the flow, and it felt incredible.

The next morning, Sally arrived at the office early, eager to dive into the world of cumulative flow diagrams. As she approached the Kanban board, she noticed something different. The team had added a new column labeled "Continuous Improvement Ideas."

Curious, she leaned in to read some of the sticky notes:

"Automate repetitive testing tasks" "Create a knowledge base for common issues" "Implement code review checklist"

Sally felt a surge of pride. The team wasn't just following the Kanban process; they were actively looking for ways to make it better. They had truly embraced the spirit of continuous improvement.

As she sipped her coffee and contemplated the new ideas, Sally couldn't help but feel excited about what the future held. They had optimized their flow, but there was still so much to learn and improve.

"Well, Kanban," she murmured to herself, "what adventure do you have in store for us next?"

Little did Sally know, the biggest challenges – and the most rewarding breakthroughs – were yet to come. But for now, she was content to bask in the glow of their progress, ready to tackle whatever flow-related puzzles Chris had up his sleeve.

The journey from chaos to flow was well underway, and Sally couldn't wait to see where it would take them next.

Manav's Thoughts:

At this stage, Sally's team is starting to focus on optimizing their workflow. A key advanced concept that can help them here is **Bottleneck Management**. Bottlenecks are points in the workflow where work accumulates and slows down the entire process. Identifying and addressing bottlenecks can drastically improve the team's flow and efficiency.

For Sally's team, they might notice that tasks tend to get stuck in the testing phase because there aren't enough testers or because testing resources are shared across multiple teams. To address this, the team could implement strategies like **Cross-Training** team members to perform testing or **Reallocating Resources** to ensure that there's enough capacity at the bottleneck stage to keep work flowing smoothly.

From a practical standpoint, bottleneck management is about continuously monitoring the system, identifying where work is getting stuck, and taking steps to alleviate the pressure. This prevents bottlenecks from becoming a recurring issue and helps maintain a steady flow of work.

For further reading on Bottleneck Management and how to address them, check out:

- "The Bottleneck Rules: How to Get More Done (When Working Harder Isn't Working)" by Clarke Ching
- "The Principles of Product Development Flow: Second Generation Lean Product Development" by Donald G. Reinertsen

These books provide practical strategies for identifying and eliminating bottlenecks, helping teams maintain a steady flow of work.

Chapter 8

Feedback Loops: The Key to Continuous Improvement

Sally stared at her reflection in the bathroom mirror, toothbrush in hand, and narrowed her eyes critically. "Hmm," she muttered, "Left molar brushing efficiency seems to have decreased by 2% since yesterday. Must adjust technique."

She paused, toothbrush midair, and burst out laughing. "Oh god," she groaned, "I'm doing it again, aren't I?"

Ever since the team had started implementing daily standups and regular retrospectives at work, Sally had found herself applying the concept of feedback loops to every aspect of her life. It had started innocently enough — a little self-reflection here, a progress check there. But now? Now she was analyzing her tooth-brushing technique with the intensity of a NASA engineer preparing for a moon launch.

As she finished getting ready for work, Sally couldn't help but chuckle at her own obsessiveness. Still, she had to admit that the increased focus on feedback and continuous improvement had been transformative for the team. Their Kanban journey had taken an interesting turn with the introduction of these structured feedback sessions.

Arriving at the office, Sally found the team already gathered around the Kanban board for their daily standup. Chris, their resident Kanban guru, was facilitating today's meeting.

"Alright, team," Chris began, "let's keep this focused and efficient. We'll go around the board, discussing any blocked items and opportunities for improvement. Remember, this isn't a status update – it's about identifying and removing obstacles to our flow."

Sally nodded approvingly. They'd come a long way from their first few standups, which had often devolved into lengthy status reports or tangential discussions about the latest office gossip.

Dave, the lead developer, spoke up first. "I've got a blocked item in the 'In Progress' column," he said, pointing to a red-flagged sticky note. "The new feature is waiting on input from the UX team before I can proceed."

Tina from QA chimed in, "I can help with that. I was just talking to Alex from UX yesterday about a similar issue. I'll connect you two after the standup."

Sally watched as Chris deftly guided the conversation, keeping it focused on removing blockers and improving flow. It was a far cry from their early attempts at standups, which had often left team members more confused and frustrated than when they started.

As the standup wrapped up, Sally reflected on how much more productive these sessions had become. By using the Kanban board as a visual aid and sticking to a strict time limit, they were able to quickly identify and address issues without getting bogged down in unnecessary details.

Later that day, as Sally was refilling her coffee mug, she overheard Dave and Tina chatting by the water cooler.

"You know," Dave was saying, "I used to dread these daily standups. They felt like a waste of time. But now? I actually look forward to them. It's like we're all working together to solve a giant puzzle."

Tina nodded enthusiastically. "I know what you mean. And have you noticed how much quicker we are to catch and fix issues now? It's like we've developed a sixth sense for potential problems."

Sally smiled to herself, pleased to see how the team had embraced the feedback loop mentality. But their journey wasn't over yet. Today was also the day of their bi-weekly retrospective, and she had a feeling it was going to be an interesting one.

As the team gathered in the conference room that afternoon, there was an air of anticipation. These retrospectives had become a crucial part of their continuous improvement process, and everyone knew that big changes often stemmed from these sessions.

"Alright, team," Sally began, taking on the role of facilitator for this retrospective. "Let's start with what's been working well since our last meeting. Any victories to celebrate?"

The room buzzed with positive energy as team members shared their wins. Improved communication between developers and testers, faster resolution of blocked items, and a noticeable decrease in last-minute emergencies were all highlighted.

"Great stuff," Sally said, jotting down notes on the whiteboard. "Now, let's move on to areas where we think we can improve. Remember, this isn't about pointing fingers – it's about identifying opportunities to make our process even better."

The mood in the room shifted slightly as people began to voice their concerns and frustrations. But unlike in the past, where such discussions might have devolved into blame games or defensive posturing, the team approached these issues with a spirit of collaborative problem-solving.

"I've noticed that our 'Ready for QA' column often becomes a bottleneck," Tina said. "It seems like we're not quite prepared for the testing phase when items reach that stage."

Dave nodded in agreement. "You're right. I think part of the problem is that we're not always clear on the acceptance criteria for each task. Maybe we need to revisit how we're defining 'Done' for our development phase?"

As the discussion continued, a pattern began to emerge. The team realized that while their overall flow had improved dramatically, there were still gaps in their definition and communication of acceptance criteria at various stages of their process.

"I think we've identified our focus for the next two weeks," Sally said, summarizing the key points on the whiteboard. "We need to create clearer, more comprehensive acceptance criteria for each stage of our workflow. This should help reduce bottlenecks and improve the quality of our deliverables."

The team left the retrospective energized and focused, each member clear on their role in implementing this improvement. As Sally erased the whiteboard, she couldn't help but feel a sense of pride in how far they'd come. These feedback loops – the daily standups and regular retrospectives – had become the engine driving their continuous improvement.

That evening, as Sally prepared dinner in her kitchen, she found herself applying the lessons from work to her cooking process. She'd been trying to improve her culinary skills, and realized that she could benefit from some structured feedback loops here too.

"Okay, Schrödinger," she said to her cat, who was watching her culinary efforts with typical feline skepticism, "time for our daily standup. Any blockers to report in Operation Dinner?"

Schrödinger blinked slowly, which Sally chose to interpret as, "The chicken seems overcooked, and you forgot to buy fresh herbs again."

"Fair points," Sally nodded, making a mental note to set a timer for the chicken next time and add herbs to her shopping list. "Any other feedback?"

Schrödinger yawned and stretched, which Sally took as a sign that the standup was over. She chuckled to herself, realizing how ingrained the feedback loop mentality had become in her thinking.

As she sat down to enjoy her slightly overcooked but steadily improving dinner, Sally reflected on the power of these continuous feedback mechanisms. At work, they had transformed a chaotic, reactive team into a proactive, continuously improving unit. And in her personal life, well... she might be taking it a bit too far with the tooth-brushing analysis, but overall, the increased mindfulness and regular self-reflection were having a positive impact.

The next morning, as the team gathered for their daily standup, Sally noticed a new energy in the room. Everyone seemed more engaged, more focused on identifying and solving problems proactively.

"I've been thinking about our acceptance criteria issue," Dave said as they discussed the 'In Progress' column. "I've drafted a template we could use to ensure we're capturing all the necessary information before moving items to 'Ready for QA'. Could we review it together later today?"

Tina's face lit up. "That would be fantastic! I'd love to provide input from a testing perspective."

Sally watched with pride as her team members took ownership of the improvement process. This was the power of effective feedback loops in action – not only were they identifying issues, but they were also actively working on solutions without needing to be prompted.

As the standup concluded, Chris pulled Sally aside. "I'm impressed," he said, nodding towards the team as they dispersed to their desks. "They've really embraced the concept of continuous improvement. But I'm sensing there might be a new challenge on the horizon. Care to grab a coffee and chat about it?"

Sally raised an eyebrow, intrigued. "New challenge? Do tell."

Over coffee, Chris explained his observation. "The team is doing great with identifying and implementing small improvements. But I'm wondering if we're missing opportunities for larger, more transformative changes. Sometimes, continuous improvement can lead to local optimization at the expense of global optimization."

Sally furrowed her brow, considering Chris's words. "You're right," she said slowly. "We've been so focused on tweaking our current process that we haven't really stepped back to consider if there might be entirely new approaches we could take."

Chris nodded. "Exactly. Don't get me wrong – the small, incremental improvements are crucial. But every now and then, it's important to zoom out and consider more radical changes."

As they continued to discuss this new perspective, Sally felt a familiar spark of excitement. Just when she thought she had a handle on this Kanban thing, a new layer of complexity and opportunity revealed itself.

Returning to her desk, Sally found herself lost in thought. How could they incorporate this idea of balancing small improvements with potentially larger, more disruptive changes? As she pondered this question, her eyes fell on the "Continuous Improvement Ideas" column they had added to their Kanban board a few weeks ago.

Suddenly, an idea struck her. What if they added another column next to it, something like "Blue Sky Ideas"? A place for team members to suggest more radical, out-of-the-box solutions that might not fit into their current incremental improvement model?

Excited by the possibility, Sally quickly sketched out her idea and sent a message to the team, calling for a quick huddle.

As she explained her concept to the gathered team members, she could see the spark of interest in their eyes. This new column could be a breeding ground for innovation, a place where they could dream big without the constraints of their current process.

"I love it," Dave said, nodding enthusiastically. "Sometimes I have ideas that seem too big or different to fit into our regular improvement cycle. This would give us a place to capture those thoughts."

Tina chimed in, "And who knows? Maybe some of those wild ideas could lead to breakthrough improvements we wouldn't have considered otherwise."

The team quickly agreed to implement the new column, and within minutes, sticky notes with bold, ambitious ideas began to populate the space. Sally couldn't help but feel a sense of pride and excitement. They had taken a potential limitation of their process and turned it into an opportunity for growth and innovation.

As the day wound down, Sally found herself once again reflecting on their Kanban journey. What had started as a simple board with sticky notes had evolved into a powerful system for continuous improvement and innovation. The daily standups, regular retrospectives, and now this new avenue for big-picture thinking were all working together to drive their team forward.

She thought back to the chaotic, overwhelmed group they had been just a few months ago. The transformation was remarkable. Yes, they still faced challenges, and yes, there was always room for improvement. But they now had the tools and mindset to tackle those challenges head-on.

As she packed up her things to head home, Sally's phone buzzed with a message from Chris: "Great idea with the Blue Sky column. Ready to dive into some advanced Kanban concepts tomorrow? I think it's time we talked about Classes of Service."

Sally grinned, already anticipating the new insights and challenges that lay ahead. "Bring it on," she typed back. "I have a feeling our Kanban adventure is just getting started."

Walking out of the office, Sally couldn't help but feel a sense of excitement about what the future held. They had mastered the art of feedback loops and continuous improvement, but there was still so much to learn and explore in the world of Kanban.

As she stepped onto the bus for her commute home, Sally found herself automatically analyzing the efficiency of the boarding process, considering how Kanban principles might improve city transit. She chuckled to herself, realizing that her Kanban mindset had truly permeated every aspect of her life.

"Well, Kanban," she muttered under her breath, earning a curious glance from her seatmate, "looks like you and I are in this for the long haul. I can't wait to see where we go next."

Little did Sally know, the journey from chaos to flow was far from over. The biggest challenges – and the most rewarding breakthroughs – were yet to come. But for now, she was content in the knowledge that they had built a solid foundation of continuous improvement, driven by the power of effective feedback loops.

The Kanban adventure continued, and Sally was ready for whatever came next.

Manav's Thoughts:

Feedback loops are essential for continuous improvement in Kanban, and Sally's team has already begun implementing them through standups and retrospectives. An advanced concept that can take these feedback loops to the next level is **Kanban Cadences**—a set of regular meetings that provide structure to the improvement process.

Kanban Cadences include several key events, such as:

- **Daily Standups** for discussing progress and blockers.
- **Service Delivery Reviews** to assess how well the team is meeting customer expectations.
- **Operations Reviews** to look at the bigger picture of how Kanban is functioning across the organization.

Sally's team could benefit from implementing these cadences to ensure that feedback is gathered regularly, both on a day-to-day basis and at a more strategic level. This would help them make incremental improvements continuously and keep the team aligned with their goals.

To learn more about Kanban Cadences and their practical applications, consider reading:

- "Kanban: Successful Evolutionary Change for Your Technology Business" by David J. Anderson
- "Kanban Maturity Model" by David J. Anderson & Teodora Bozheva

These resources provide a deeper dive into the different cadences and how they help teams stay focused on continuous improvement and customer satisfaction.

Chapter 9

Expanding Horizons: Kanban Beyond the Team

Sally strutted into the office, a spring in her step and a gleam in her eye. The team's Kanban board was a thing of beauty - a well-oiled machine of productivity and flow. As she approached, she overheard snippets of conversation from her teammates.

"Did you see how quickly that last feature moved through testing?" Tina from QA was saying, her voice tinged with excitement.

Dave, the lead developer, nodded enthusiastically. "I know! And the best part is, no last-minute fire drills or overtime. We actually finished early!"

Sally couldn't help but grin. Their Kanban journey had transformed not just their workflow, but the entire team dynamic. Gone were the days of chaos and constant firefighting. They were now a model of efficiency and collaboration.

As she settled at her desk, Sally's inbox pinged with a new message. It was from Brad in Marketing - the same Brad who used to burst into their office with "urgent" requests that threw their entire schedule into disarray. She opened the email with a mix of curiosity and trepidation.

"Hey Sally," the message read, "I've been hearing great things about what your team has been doing with this Kanban thing. Any chance you could come by and show us how it works? We're drowning in campaigns and could use some of that organization magic!"

Sally leaned back in her chair, a bemused expression on her face. Brad wanting to learn about Kanban? It seemed the world really was full of surprises.

"What's got you looking so thoughtful?" Chris asked, appearing at her desk with his ever-present cup of coffee.

Sally showed him Brad's email. "Looks like our Kanban success is spreading. Marketing wants in on the action."

Chris's eyes lit up. "That's fantastic! It's a great opportunity to see how Kanban can adapt to different workflows." He paused, a mischievous grin spreading across his face. "Plus, it'll be interesting to see how Brad handles having his work visualized on a board for all to see."

Sally couldn't help but chuckle at the thought. "True. But how do we even start? Their workflow is so different from ours."

Chris nodded sagely. "That's the beauty of Kanban - it's flexible. We just need to help them map their own process. Why don't we set up a workshop with their team?"

Over the next few days, Sally found herself diving deep into the world of marketing workflows. She and Chris spent hours with Brad and his team, mapping out their processes, identifying bottlenecks, and translating their work into a Kanban system that made sense for them.

It wasn't always smooth sailing. There were heated debates about what constituted a "task" in marketing, and how to handle long-running campaigns versus quick social media posts. But slowly, surely, a marketing Kanban board began to take shape.

"So, let me get this straight," Brad said during one of their sessions, squinting at the board they'd created. "Each campaign is a swimlane, and we move the tasks for that campaign across the board?"

Sally nodded encouragingly. "Exactly! And see these WIP limits at the top of each column? They'll help prevent any one stage from getting overloaded."

Brad's brow furrowed. "But what if we have a rush job from the CEO? We can't just say no because of some arbitrary limit, can we?"

Sally and Chris exchanged knowing glances. They'd had this exact conversation in their own team months ago.

"Actually, Brad," Chris interjected gently, "that's exactly what you should do. But don't worry - we'll show you how to handle expedited items without throwing your entire system into chaos."

As the marketing team's Kanban system took shape, Sally couldn't help but feel a sense of déjà vu. The questions, the resistance, the gradual shift in mindset - it was all eerily familiar. But there was also something deeply satisfying about seeing Kanban principles applied in a completely different context.

Energized by the success with the marketing team, Sally found herself looking for other areas where she could apply Kanban principles. Her gaze fell on her home life, which was still a bit of a mess despite her best efforts.

That evening, she arrived home with a determined glint in her eye and a bag full of sticky notes and markers. Her roommate, Alex, looked up from the couch, a mix of curiosity and concern on his face.

"Uh oh," Alex said, eyeing the supplies. "I know that look. What crazy scheme are you cooking up now?"

Sally grinned, already envisioning a Kanban board covering their living room wall. "Oh, nothing much. Just thought we could use a little organization around here. How do you feel about visualizing our household chores?"

What followed was a weekend of what Sally optimistically called "domestic Kanban implementation" and what Alex referred to as "Sally's descent into sticky note madness."

They created a board for household chores, complete with swimlanes for each roommate and columns for different stages of task completion. Sally was in her element, enthusiastically explaining WIP limits and the pull system to an increasingly bewildered Alex.

"So, I can't start a new task until I've finished the one I'm working on?" Alex asked, staring at the colorful array of sticky notes.

"Exactly!" Sally beamed. "It'll help us avoid having a bunch of half-done chores lying around."

Alex nodded slowly, a hint of amusement in his eyes. "Right. Because that was totally our biggest problem. Not the fact that we both work crazy hours and sometimes forget to buy toilet paper."

Despite Alex's gentle ribbing, they gave the system a try. And while it didn't magically transform their apartment into a spotless paradise, it did lead to some improvements. They were more aware of what needed to be done, and there was less bickering about who had done what.

But Sally also learned a valuable lesson about scaling systems - what worked perfectly for her didn't necessarily translate seamlessly to others. Alex found some aspects of the system helpful but chafed at others. They had to adapt and adjust, finding a middle ground that worked for both of them.

Back at work, the success of the marketing team's Kanban implementation had caught the attention of upper management. Sally found herself in a meeting with the CEO, Frank, explaining the basics of Kanban and how it had transformed their team's productivity.

Frank listened intently, occasionally interrupting with sharp questions that showed he was really engaging with the concept. As Sally wrapped up her presentation, Frank leaned back in his chair, a thoughtful expression on his face.

"This is impressive stuff, Sally," he said. "But here's my question - can we scale this up? We've got a major project coming up that involves multiple teams across different departments. Could Kanban help us manage that?"

Sally felt a mix of excitement and trepidation. This was a huge opportunity, but also a massive challenge. She glanced at Chris, who gave her an encouraging nod.

"It's definitely possible, Frank," Sally said, her mind already racing with ideas. "But it would require careful planning and coordination. We'd need to create a system that allows for team-level autonomy while also providing visibility and alignment at the project level."

Frank's eyes lit up. "That sounds exactly like what we need. Can you put together a proposal? I want to see how we could implement this for our upcoming product launch."

As Sally left the meeting, her head was spinning with possibilities and potential pitfalls. Scaling Kanban to a multi-team, multi-department project was a whole new ball game.

Over the next few weeks, Sally and Chris worked tirelessly to design a scaled Kanban system for the product launch project. They met with team leads from every department involved, mapping out workflows, identifying dependencies, and creating a structure that would allow for both team-level management and project-wide visibility.

It was during one of these planning sessions that Sally had an epiphany. They were discussing how to handle dependencies between teams when she suddenly thought of her and Alex's chore board at home.

"What if we treat each team like we treated roommates in our home Kanban system?" she mused aloud. "They each have their own swimlane, but there's a shared space for tasks that affect multiple teams."

Chris's eyes lit up. "Brilliant! And we could use different colored cards for each department, making it easy to see at a glance where work is coming from and going to."

As their multi-team Kanban system took shape, Sally was struck by how much she had learned since their journey began. The principles remained the same, but the application had to be flexible, adapting to the unique needs and challenges of each context.

The day finally came to present their scaled Kanban proposal to Frank and the other executives. Sally stood in front of the room, feeling a mixture of nervousness and excitement.

"Ladies and gentlemen," she began, "what you're looking at is a Kanban system designed to manage our entire product launch project."

She walked them through the system, explaining how each team had its own board that fed into a higher-level project board. She showed how they could track dependencies, manage shared resources, and maintain visibility across the entire project.

As she spoke, Sally could see the executives leaning forward, their eyes moving across the complex yet intuitive system she and Chris had designed. When she finished, there was a moment of silence.

Then Frank stood up, a broad smile on his face. "Sally, Chris, this is outstanding work. I can already see how this will transform our project management. Let's roll it out immediately."

As they left the meeting, Chris nudged Sally's shoulder. "Look at you, Kanban rock star. We've come a long way from that chaotic team board, huh?"

Sally laughed, shaking her head in amazement. "We certainly have. Though I have to say, I never expected Kanban to take over my whole life like this. I'm pretty sure I even dream in swimlanes now."

Chris grinned. "Welcome to the club. Just wait until you start seeing Kanban principles in nature. That's when you know you're really hooked."

As they walked back to their desks, Sally found herself reflecting on their Kanban journey. From a single team struggling with chaos to a company-wide system managing complex projects - it had been quite a ride.

She thought about the marketing team, proudly showing off their board in their latest team meeting. She thought about Alex, who had begrudgingly admitted that their home Kanban system had made life a little easier. And she thought about all the teams across the company who were about to embark on their own Kanban adventures.

There were sure to be challenges ahead. Scaling any system across an organization was never easy. But Sally felt confident that the flexibility and power of Kanban would see them through.

As she settled at her desk, her phone buzzed with a message from Chris: "Ready for our next challenge? I hear HR is interested in Kanban for their recruitment process..."

Sally couldn't help but laugh. It seemed their Kanban journey was far from over. In fact, it felt like they were just getting started.

She typed back a quick reply: "Bring it on! But first, I need to update our team board. We've got a whole new project to plan!"

As she stood up to approach their team's Kanban board, Sally felt a surge of excitement. They had come so far, learned so much, but there was still a world of possibilities to explore. Kanban had transformed not just their work, but their entire approach to problem-solving and continuous improvement.

The journey from chaos to flow was ongoing, constantly evolving. And Sally couldn't wait to see where it would take them next.

Little did she know, the biggest challenges - and the most rewarding breakthroughs - were yet to come. But for now, she was content in the knowledge that they had built a solid foundation, not just for their team, but for the entire company.

The Kanban revolution was spreading, and Sally was leading the charge.

Manav's Thoughts:

In this chapter, Sally's team begins to scale Kanban beyond their immediate team to other departments. This is a great time to introduce **Upstream and Downstream Kanban**. Upstream Kanban focuses on managing work before it enters the team's workflow, such as prioritizing incoming requests or grooming a backlog. Downstream Kanban manages how work is completed and delivered to the customer.

For Sally's team, implementing upstream Kanban could help them manage incoming work more effectively. For example, they could work with stakeholders to prioritize requests and ensure that only work that is ready to be pulled into the development cycle enters the system. This prevents the team from being overwhelmed by incomplete or poorly defined tasks.

Downstream Kanban, on the other hand, helps manage the final stages of work, ensuring that delivery to the customer is smooth and that feedback loops are closed properly. This would help Sally's team deliver higher-quality products faster and with fewer issues.

For more on Upstream and Downstream Kanban, check out:

- "Fit for Purpose: How Modern Businesses Find, Satisfy, & Keep Customers" by David J. Anderson & Alexei Zheglov
- "Actionable Agile Metrics for Predictability" by Daniel S. Vacanti

These books offer insights into how upstream and downstream Kanban help align the entire organization around delivering value to customers.

Chapter 10

The Customer Connection

Sally stared at her computer screen, a mixture of pride and trepidation swirling in her stomach. The email from their biggest client, MegaCorp, glowed on the screen:

"Dear Sally and team, We're impressed with the recent improvements in your responsiveness and product quality. We'd like to schedule a meeting to discuss expanding our partnership..."

"Well, would you look at that," Chris's voice startled her out of her reverie. "Seems like our Kanban magic is working its charms on the customers too."

Sally grinned, spinning in her chair to face her mentor. "I know! It's amazing how much has changed. Remember when we used to dread client emails because they always meant fire drills and overtime?"

Chris chuckled, perching on the edge of her desk. "Oh, I remember. The good old days of chaos and panic. So, what's the plan for this meeting?"

Sally's grin faltered slightly. "That's the thing. I was thinking... maybe we could use this as an opportunity to integrate customer feedback more directly into our Kanban system?"

Chris's eyebrows shot up, a spark of interest lighting his eyes. "Now that's an intriguing idea. Tell me more."

Over the next hour, Sally and Chris huddled at her desk, sketching out ideas for incorporating customer input into their Kanban workflow. By the time they were done, Sally's notepad was covered in scribbles, arrows, and enough sticky notes to make a stationary store jealous.

"Okay, let me see if I've got this straight," Chris said, leaning back and rubbing his eyes. "We create a new swim lane on our board for customer requests, with its own WIP limit to ensure we're always working on something customer-facing without neglecting our other work?"

Sally nodded enthusiastically. "Exactly! And we set up a regular cadence for reviewing and prioritizing these requests with the customer. That way, we're not just reacting to whatever seems most urgent in the moment."

Chris smiled, a mixture of pride and amusement on his face. "Look at you, all grown up and innovating our Kanban system. I think we're onto something here."

The next morning, Sally presented their idea to the team. To her relief, everyone seemed excited about the prospect of working more closely with their customers.

"I love it," Tina from QA said. "Maybe this will help us catch potential issues before they become full-blown problems."

Dave, the lead developer, nodded in agreement. "And it'll be nice to have a clearer picture of what features the customers actually want, instead of just guessing."

As they began implementing the new customer feedback lane, Sally couldn't help but feel a sense of excitement. This felt like the missing piece in their Kanban puzzle – a direct line to the people they were ultimately trying to serve.

Of course, as with any new process, there were some teething problems. The team quickly realized that not all customer requests were created equal. Some were simple bug fixes that could be knocked out in an afternoon, while others were complex feature requests that would take weeks to implement.

"We need a way to categorize these requests," Sally mused during one of their daily stand-ups. "Something that helps us balance the quick wins with the longer-term projects."

Chris snapped his fingers. "What about using different colored sticky notes? Green for quick fixes, yellow for medium-complexity tasks, and red for major feature requests?"

The team loved the idea, and soon their customer request lane was a rainbow of prioritized tasks. It was visually appealing and instantly informative – anyone could glance at the board and get a sense of the customer work in progress.

As the weeks went by, the benefits of their new system became increasingly apparent. Customer satisfaction scores were on the rise, and the team found themselves spending less time putting out fires and more time proactively addressing customer needs.

But the real test came on a Tuesday afternoon, when Sally's phone rang with a call from their MegaCorp contact, Steve.

"Sally, we've got a situation," Steve's voice was tense. "Our system just went down, and we're losing thousands of dollars every minute. We need a fix ASAP."

In the past, this kind of call would have thrown the entire team into panic mode. But now, Sally felt a strange sense of calm. "I understand, Steve. Let me check our board and get back to you in five minutes."

She hung up and hurried to the Kanban board. The team was already gathered, having overheard her conversation.

"Alright, team," Sally said, her voice steady. "We've got an urgent customer issue. Here's what we're going to do."

With practiced efficiency, they created a new red sticky note for the MegaCorp emergency and placed it in their expedite lane. Dave immediately pulled the task, while Tina cleared her current work to be ready for immediate testing.

Within minutes, they had a plan of action. Sally called Steve back, outlining their response and estimated timeline. "We'll have a fix to you within the hour, Steve. I'll keep you updated every 15 minutes on our progress."

True to her word, Sally provided regular updates to Steve. The team worked with focused intensity, and in just 47 minutes, they had identified the issue, developed a fix, tested it, and deployed it to MegaCorp's system.

Steve was ecstatic. "I don't know how you did it, Sally, but you've just saved our bacon. Thank you doesn't even begin to cover it."

As Sally hung up the phone, she turned to find the entire team watching her, grins on their faces.

"Now that," Chris said, slow clapping, "is how you handle a customer emergency."

The team burst into cheers and high fives. They had faced a major challenge and come through with flying colors, all thanks to their Kanban system and their new customer-focused approach.

Riding high on their success at work, Sally decided it was time to apply some Kanban principles to her personal life. With a family reunion looming on the horizon, she thought it would be the perfect opportunity to test out her customer feedback skills.

That evening, she set up a family group chat, determined to gather input and create the perfect reunion plan. "Alright, family," she typed, "let's treat this reunion like a product launch. What features would you like to see?"

The responses came flooding in faster than Sally could keep up. Aunt Mildred wanted a formal sit-down dinner. Cousin Jake suggested a paintball tournament. Uncle Bob's only request was "plenty of beer".

Sally stared at her phone, her initial enthusiasm waning as she realized she had just opened Pandora's box of family opinions. "Maybe I should have set a WIP limit on suggestions," she muttered to herself.

Determined to make it work, Sally created a Kanban board on her living room wall, complete with sticky notes for each family member's requests. She even color-coded them based on complexity – green for "sure, why not?", yellow for "maybe with some tweaking", and red for "how about no, Uncle Bob, we're not having a 'who can drink the most beer' contest".

Her roommate, Alex, wandered in and stopped short at the sight of the family reunion Kanban board. "Uh, Sally? You okay there, buddy?"

Sally, surrounded by a sea of sticky notes and looking slightly manic, turned to Alex with a forced smile. "Oh, I'm great! Just applying some lean principles to family event planning. Did you know Grandma wants to do a TikTok dance challenge?"

Alex backed away slowly. "Right... I'm just gonna go... anywhere else. Good luck with your family... product launch?"

As the days went by, Sally found herself constantly reprioritizing family requests, trying to balance everyone's needs and wants. She held daily stand-up meetings with herself in front of the board, much to Alex's continued bemusement.

Finally, the day of the reunion arrived. To Sally's surprise and relief, it went off without a hitch. The Kanban-style planning had allowed her to create a balanced event that had a little something for everyone – from Aunt Mildred's formal dinner to a slightly tamer version of Cousin Jake's paintball idea (water balloons proved to be a hit with all ages).

As Sally watched her family laughing and enjoying themselves, she couldn't help but feel a sense of accomplishment. She had successfully applied Kanban principles to wrangle the chaos of family opinions into a cohesive and enjoyable event.

Back at work on Monday, Sally shared her family reunion Kanban adventure with the team, much to their amusement.

"So, what you're saying is," Dave said between chuckles, "we should treat our customers like a big, opinionated family?"

Sally laughed. "Well, when you put it that way... actually, yes! That's exactly what I'm saying. Everyone has their own priorities and ideas, but with the right system, we can balance all those needs and create something that works for everyone."

Chris nodded approvingly. "You know, that's not a bad analogy. Our job is to listen to all those diverse opinions, prioritize them effectively, and deliver a product that makes everyone happy – or at least, as happy as possible."

The team spent the rest of the day refining their customer feedback process, inspired by Sally's family reunion experience. They set up a more structured way of gathering and categorizing customer requests, created a regular schedule for review and prioritization meetings with key clients, and even developed a system for quickly prototyping and getting feedback on new features.

As the weeks went by, the results of their efforts became increasingly apparent. Customer satisfaction scores continued to climb, and they started receiving glowing feedback about their responsiveness and ability to deliver exactly what was needed.

One afternoon, as Sally was updating their metrics board, she noticed something remarkable. "Hey team," she called out, excitement in her voice, "come look at this!"

The team gathered around as Sally pointed to their lead time chart. "Our average time from customer request to delivery has decreased by 40% since we implemented our new system."

There were gasps and murmurs of appreciation from the team. Dave whistled low. "That's impressive. No wonder our customers are so happy."

Tina nodded enthusiastically. "And look at our quality metrics. Bugs reported by customers are down by 30%. We're not just delivering faster, we're delivering better."

As the team celebrated their success, Sally couldn't help but reflect on how far they'd come. From the chaos of their pre-Kanban days to this finely tuned, customer-focused machine – it was a transformation she never could have imagined when they started this journey.

Later that day, Sally received an email that made her smile from ear to ear. It was from Steve at MegaCorp:

"Dear Sally and team, I wanted to take a moment to express our gratitude for the incredible work you've been doing. Your responsiveness, the quality of your deliverables, and your ability to understand and meet our needs have exceeded all expectations. We're not just satisfied customers – we're fans. We'd like to discuss expanding our contract and making you our primary software partner across all our divisions..."

As Sally shared the email with the team, the office erupted in cheers. This was more than just a business success – it was validation of everything they'd worked so hard to achieve.

Chris appeared at Sally's side, a proud smile on his face. "Well done, Sally. You've taken Kanban and turned it into a true competitive advantage."

Sally beamed, but then a thought struck her. "You know, Chris, I was just thinking... if we can do this for external customers, imagine what we could do if we applied the same principles to our internal processes? HR, Finance, Operations – they're all our customers too, in a way."

Chris's eyes lit up with that familiar spark of excitement. "Now that's an interesting idea. Care to sketch out some thoughts on the board?"

As they walked towards their Kanban board, already deep in discussion about how to extend their customer-focused approach across the entire organization, Sally felt a sense of excitement about what the future held.

They had mastered the art of connecting with customers through Kanban, but there was still so much more to explore and improve. The journey from chaos to flow was ongoing, constantly evolving, and Sally couldn't wait to see where it would take them next.

Little did she know, the biggest challenges – and the most rewarding breakthroughs – were yet to come. But for now, she was content in the knowledge that they had built a system that not only improved their work but also genuinely delighted their customers.

The Kanban revolution was changing not just how they worked, but how they connected with the very people they were working for. And Sally was leading the charge, one sticky note at a time.

Manav's Thoughts:

In this chapter, Sally's team begins to incorporate customer feedback more directly into their Kanban system. An advanced concept that complements this is **Lead Time Distribution Charts**. These charts help teams analyze how long different types of tasks take to complete, based on historical data. This data can then be used to set realistic expectations for customers and improve planning accuracy.

For Sally's team, introducing lead time distribution charts would allow them to predict how long future work might take, giving them a better understanding of their workflow and helping them meet customer expectations more consistently. This is especially important when handling feature requests or bug fixes that have different urgency levels.

From a practical standpoint, tracking lead times helps teams identify patterns in their work and make more informed decisions about prioritization and resource allocation.

To learn more about Lead Time Distribution and its application in Kanban, I recommend:

- **"When Will It Be Done? Lean-Agile Forecasting to Answer Your Customers' Most Important Question" by Daniel S. Vacanti**
- **"Agile Estimating and Planning" by Mike Cohn**

These books explore how tracking lead times and using historical data can lead to better predictability and planning in Kanban.

Chapter 11

Kanban 2.0: Advanced Techniques

Sally stared at the Kanban board, her brow furrowed in concentration. The once-simple board had evolved into a complex ecosystem of sticky notes, swim lanes, and color-coded tags. It was beautiful, in a chaotic sort of way, like a Jackson Pollock painting made of productivity.

"Admiring your handiwork?" Chris's voice startled her out of her reverie.

Sally chuckled, shaking her head. "More like wondering if we've created a monster. Look at this, Chris. We've got feature requests, bug fixes, technical debt, and who knows what else all competing for attention. How do we prioritize?"

Chris grinned, a mischievous glint in his eye. "Ah, my young Padawan. It's time for you to learn the ways of Kanban 2.0."

"Kanban 2.0?" Sally raised an eyebrow. "Is that like Web 2.0, but with more sticky notes?"

Chris laughed. "Not quite. It's about taking Kanban to the next level. And I think I know just the technique to help with our current predicament. Have you ever heard of Class of Service?"

Sally's blank stare was all the answer he needed.

"Right," Chris continued, "think of it as a way to categorize work based on urgency and importance. It helps us handle different types of work more effectively."

As Chris explained the concept, Sally's mind began to race with possibilities. They spent the next hour huddled at the board, sketching out ideas for how to implement Class of Service in their workflow.

The next morning, Sally called the team together for a special meeting. "Alright, gang," she began, barely containing her excitement, "we're about to level up our Kanban game."

She explained the concept of Class of Service, outlining four categories they'd be using:

1. **Expedite:** For urgent, high-impact items that need immediate attention.
2. **Fixed Delivery Date:** For items with a specific deadline.
3. **Standard:** For regular, day-to-day work.
4. **Intangible:** For items that add value but aren't time-sensitive, like paying down technical debt.

The team listened intently, a mix of curiosity and skepticism on their faces.

Dave, the lead developer, was the first to speak up. "So, how does this actually work in practice? Do we just slap a label on each task and call it a day?"

Sally grinned. "Not quite, Dave. We're going to set up different policies for each class. For example, Expedite items automatically jump to the front of the queue and have no WIP limit. But we'll only allow one Expedite item at a time to prevent abuse."

Tina from QA nodded approvingly. "I like it. This could help us balance those pesky bug fixes with our feature development work."

Over the next few days, the team worked to implement their new Class of Service system. They created new swim lanes on their board, established policies for each class, and even developed a color-coding system that made the board look like a technicolor dream coat.

As they settled into their new workflow, Sally couldn't help but feel a sense of pride. They had taken Kanban and turned it into a finely-tuned machine, capable of handling the complex demands of their work.

Energized by their success at work, Sally decided it was time to apply these advanced Kanban techniques to her personal life. Armed with a fresh pack of sticky notes and more enthusiasm than common sense, she set out to optimize her home life.

That weekend, her roommate Alex walked into their living room to find every surface covered in color-coded sticky notes. Sally stood in the middle of the chaos, a marker tucked behind her ear and a manic gleam in her eye.

"Uh, Sally?" Alex ventured cautiously. "What's going on? Did the sticky note factory explode?"

Sally whirled around, grinning from ear to ear. "Alex! Perfect timing. I'm implementing a Class of Service system for our household chores. See, the red notes are Expedite tasks - things like 'buy more toilet paper' or 'fix the leaky faucet'. Yellow is for Fixed Delivery Date - like paying rent or renewing our Netflix subscription. Green is for Standard tasks, your everyday cleaning and maintenance. And blue? That's for Intangible tasks, like organizing the spice rack or color-coding our bookshelf."

Alex stared at her, mouth agape. "You've... color-coded our bookshelf?"

Sally waved dismissively. "Not yet, that's a blue task. Low priority. But look!" She pointed to a red sticky note on the fridge. "We're almost out of milk. That's an Expedite task. It automatically jumps to the top of our to-do list!"

Alex shook his head, a mixture of amusement and concern on his face. "Sally, don't you think this is a bit... much? I mean, do we really need a complex system to remember to buy milk?"

Sally's enthusiasm dimmed slightly. "Well, when you put it like that..." She looked around at the sea of sticky notes, suddenly seeing the absurdity of it all. "Oh god, I've gone off the deep end, haven't I?"

Alex chuckled, patting her on the shoulder. "Just a little. But hey, at least our chores are very... colorful now?"

As they worked together to peel off the excess sticky notes, Sally couldn't help but laugh at herself. "I guess there is such a thing as too much optimization, huh?"

Back at work on Monday, Sally shared her overzealous home Kanban adventure with the team, much to their amusement.

"So," Dave said between chuckles, "what you're saying is, we shouldn't color-code the office bookshelf?"

Sally grinned sheepishly. "Maybe we should focus on more pressing matters. Speaking of which, Chris mentioned something about Cumulative Flow Diagrams. Anyone know what those are about?"

Chris's eyes lit up. "Ah, CFDs! My favorite topic. Gather 'round, team. It's time for a little data visualization magic."

Over the next hour, Chris walked the team through the basics of Cumulative Flow Diagrams. Sally watched in fascination as he demonstrated how to create one using their team's data.

"Think of it as a visual representation of your work over time," Chris explained. "The width of each band shows you how much work is in each state, and the slopes tell you about your flow and cycle time."

As the team pored over their first CFD, insights began to emerge. They could see where work was piling up, where their flow was smooth, and where they had capacity issues.

"This is incredible," Sally murmured, her eyes glued to the diagram. "It's like a bird's-eye view of our entire process."

Tina nodded enthusiastically. "Look here," she pointed to a widening band on the chart. "This shows where we started accumulating a backlog in testing. If we'd had this earlier, we could have caught that bottleneck much sooner."

The team spent the rest of the day diving deep into CFDs, learning how to create and interpret them. By the end of the week, they had set up automated CFD generation for their project, providing a daily snapshot of their workflow health.

As Sally updated their Kanban board one evening, adding the day's data to their CFD, she couldn't help but marvel at how far they'd come. From a simple board with three columns to this sophisticated system with Class of Service, explicit policies, and data-driven insights – it was a transformation she never could have imagined when they started this journey.

Chris appeared at her elbow, two steaming cups of coffee in hand. "Penny for your thoughts?"

Sally accepted the coffee gratefully. "Just thinking about how much we've evolved. Remember when we thought a sticky note with 'Urgent!' scrawled on it was advanced task management?"

Chris chuckled. "We've come a long way, that's for sure. But you know what the best part is? We're not done yet. There's always room for improvement, always new techniques to explore."

Sally nodded, taking a sip of her coffee. "You're right. In fact, I've been thinking... now that we have all this data from our CFDs, what if we used it to forecast future performance? We could potentially predict when we'll complete certain projects or identify upcoming bottlenecks before they happen."

Chris's eyes lit up with that familiar spark of excitement. "Now that's an interesting idea. Care to brainstorm on the board?"

As they walked towards their Kanban board, already deep in discussion about statistical flow forecasting and Monte Carlo simulations, Sally felt a surge of excitement about what the future held.

They had mastered the basics of Kanban, tackled advanced techniques, and were now venturing into the realm of predictive analytics. The journey from chaos to flow was ongoing, constantly evolving, and Sally couldn't wait to see where it would take them next.

Little did she know, the biggest challenges — and the most rewarding breakthroughs — were yet to come. But for now, she was content in the knowledge that they had built a system that not only improved their work but also continuously evolved to meet new challenges.

The Kanban revolution was changing not just how they worked, but how they thought about work itself. And Sally was at the forefront, armed with sticky notes, CFDs, and an insatiable curiosity for what lay ahead.

As she added one last data point to their CFD for the day, Sally couldn't help but smile. Who would have thought that a simple board with sticky notes could lead to all this? From chaos to flow, from basic to advanced, from reactive to predictive – their Kanban journey had been nothing short of transformative.

She turned off the office lights, taking one last look at their Kanban board – a testament to their growth and learning. Tomorrow would bring new challenges, new ideas, and new opportunities to improve. And thanks to Kanban, they were ready for whatever came their way.

As Sally left the office, her mind was already racing with ideas for their next Kanban evolution. The journey wasn't over – in fact, it felt like it was just beginning. And she couldn't wait to see what Kanban 3.0 might bring.

Manav's Thoughts:

As Sally's team evolves their Kanban practice, it's time to explore **Risk Management with Kanban**. This advanced concept involves identifying and managing risks within the workflow. For example, tasks that are particularly risky (e.g., critical bugs or high-stakes features) can be flagged and given special attention.

Sally's team could introduce a dedicated "Risk Management" lane on their Kanban board, where tasks with higher risks are tracked separately from regular work. This ensures that high-risk tasks receive the attention they need without derailing the flow of other work.

From a practical standpoint, managing risk proactively prevents surprises and helps teams mitigate potential issues before they escalate. It also ensures that the most critical tasks are prioritized and handled with care.

For more on Risk Management in Kanban, consider reading:

- "Risk Management in Agile Projects" by John C. Goodpasture
- "Lean Enterprise: How High Performance Organizations Innovate at Scale" by Jez Humble, Joanne Molesky, and Barry O'Reilly

These books provide a comprehensive guide to managing risk in Agile and Kanban environments, helping teams stay ahead of potential challenges.

Chapter 12

The Kanban Mindset Shift

Sally stood in front of the Kanban board, sipping her morning coffee and marveling at the colorful array of sticky notes flowing smoothly across the columns. It was hard to believe that just a year ago, this same space had been a chaotic jumble of conflicting priorities and missed deadlines.

"Admiring your handiwork?" Chris's voice broke through her reverie.

Sally turned, a wry smile on her face. "More like marveling at how far we've come. Remember when we thought Kanban was just about moving sticky notes around?"

Chris chuckled, leaning against the nearby desk. "Oh, how naive we were. Little did we know we were embarking on a journey that would change everything."

As they stood there, reminiscing about their Kanban adventure, the rest of the team began to filter in. Dave, the once-skeptical lead developer, now had a spring in his step as he approached the board to pull his first task of the day. Tina from QA was already deep in conversation with Alex from UX, discussing how they could streamline their testing process even further.

"You know," Sally mused, loud enough for the team to hear, "I've been thinking about how much Kanban has changed the way we work. But I'm curious – how has it affected you all personally?"

The team gathered around, coffee cups in hand, eager to share their experiences.

Dave was the first to speak up. "I used to dread coming to work," he admitted. "Every day felt like a losing battle against an ever-growing mountain of tasks. But now? I actually look forward to it. I know exactly what I need to focus on, and I can see the impact of my work in real-time."

Tina nodded enthusiastically. "For me, it's the work-life balance. Before Kanban, I was constantly staying late, trying to catch up on testing. Now, I leave on time every day, and I'm actually more productive."

Alex chimed in, a grin spreading across his face. "I never thought I'd say this, but Kanban has made me a better communicator. I'm more in tune with what the team needs, and I can articulate my own needs more clearly too."

As the team shared their experiences, Sally couldn't help but reflect on her own transformation. Kanban hadn't just changed how she worked – it had fundamentally shifted her entire approach to life.

She thought back to her recent vacation planning. Instead of her usual frantic scramble to book flights and accommodations, she had created a Kanban board for her trip. Each stage of planning had its own column, with clear 'Definition of Done' criteria. The result? A stress-free planning process and the most enjoyable vacation she'd had in years.

Even her fitness routine had been Kanban-ified. Gone were the days of setting unrealistic goals and beating herself up when she failed to meet them. Now, she had a personal Kanban board for her health goals, with manageable tasks flowing from 'To Do' to 'In Progress' to 'Done'. It was oddly satisfying to move a sticky note to the 'Done' column after completing a workout or sticking to her meal plan for a week.

Sally chuckled to herself, realizing how deeply Kanban had seeped into every aspect of her life. She even found herself mentally creating Kanban boards for the most mundane tasks.

Grocery shopping? That's a pull system with a WIP limit of whatever fits in her shopping cart. Laundry? A perfect example of a continuous flow process with clear 'Definition of Done' criteria (clean, dry, and put away).

"Earth to Sally," Chris's voice broke through her thoughts. "You've got that 'I'm mentally Kanban-ing something' look again."

Sally laughed, shaking her head. "Guilty as charged. I was just thinking about how Kanban has become more than just a work thing for me. It's changed how I approach everything in life."

Chris nodded knowingly. "That's the real power of Kanban. It's not just a methodology — it's a mindset. Once you start seeing the world in terms of flow and continuous improvement, there's no going back."

As the team settled into their daily stand-up, Sally noticed a new face hovering at the edge of the group. It was Mark from the sales team, looking equal parts curious and skeptical.

After the stand-up, Sally approached him. "Hey Mark, what brings you to our neck of the woods?"

Mark shuffled his feet, looking slightly embarrassed. "Well, I've been hearing a lot about this Kanban thing you guys are doing. The higher-ups are raving about how it's improved productivity and customer satisfaction. But honestly? I don't get it. How can a bunch of sticky notes make such a big difference?"

Sally smiled, remembering her own initial skepticism. "Why don't you join me for coffee? I'll give you the crash course in Kanban."

Over the next hour, Sally walked Mark through the basics of Kanban, using examples from their own team's journey. She explained how visualizing work had exposed bottlenecks they didn't even know existed, how WIP limits had dramatically reduced their lead times, and how the focus on flow had improved both the quality of their work and their job satisfaction.

As she spoke, she could see the skepticism in Mark's eyes slowly giving way to interest. By the time she got to explaining how they had integrated customer feedback into their Kanban system, Mark was leaning forward, fully engaged.

"You know," Mark said slowly, "I've been struggling with managing my sales pipeline. It always feels like I'm juggling too many leads at once, and things keep falling through the cracks. Do you think Kanban could help with that?"

Sally's eyes lit up. "Absolutely! In fact, let's sketch out a basic Kanban board for your sales process right now."

They spent the next half hour creating a simple Kanban board for Mark's sales pipeline, with columns for 'New Leads', 'Initial Contact', 'Proposal', 'Negotiation', and 'Closed'. They set WIP limits for each stage and defined clear criteria for moving a lead from one column to the next.

As they finished, Mark stared at their creation, a look of wonder on his face. "This... this could actually work. I can already see where I've been overloading myself and where I need to focus my efforts."

Sally grinned, feeling a sense of déjà vu. It was like watching her own Kanban epiphany all over again. "Welcome to the Kanban side, Mark. Trust me, your life is about to get a whole lot more organized."

As Mark left, bubbling with excitement about implementing his new sales Kanban, Sally felt a warm glow of satisfaction. She had just witnessed firsthand the transformative power of the Kanban mindset.

Later that evening, as Sally prepared dinner (using her kitchen Kanban board, of course), she found herself reflecting on the unexpected benefits Kanban had brought to her life.

Her work-life balance had improved dramatically. With clear visibility into her workload and the ability to set realistic WIP limits, she no longer felt the need to work late or on weekends. She was more productive during work hours and actually had energy left for her personal life.

Job satisfaction was at an all-time high, not just for her but for the entire team. The sense of accomplishment that came from seeing work flow smoothly across the board was addictive. They were delivering more value to their customers than ever before, and the positive feedback was a constant source of motivation.

Perhaps most surprisingly, Sally found that she had a stronger sense of control over both her work and her personal life. The chaos that had once dominated her days had given way to a sense of calm purpose. She knew what needed to be done, had a system for prioritizing and executing tasks, and could easily adapt to changes as they arose.

As she sat down to enjoy her perfectly timed dinner (thank you, kitchen Kanban), Sally couldn't help but smile. The journey from chaos to flow had been challenging at times, but the destination was worth every sticky note, every WIP limit discussion, and every retrospective.

Her phone buzzed with a message from Chris: "Hey Sally, got a new Kanban challenge for you. Ever thought about how we could apply this to our company's strategic planning process?"

Sally grinned, already feeling the familiar excitement of a new Kanban frontier to explore. "Bring it on," she typed back. "You know me – I never met a process I couldn't Kanban-ify!"

As she hit send, Sally realized that this was perhaps the biggest shift of all. She no longer saw problems – she saw opportunities for improvement. She no longer feared change – she embraced it as a chance to learn and grow. The Kanban mindset had transformed her from a stressed-out, overwhelmed business analyst into a confident, adaptable problem-solver.

She glanced at the small Kanban board on her fridge, where a sticky note in the 'To Do' column read "Write thank you note to Chris for introducing Kanban." With a smile, she moved it to 'In Progress'. It was time to acknowledge the journey that had changed everything.

As she penned the note, Sally reflected on the core principles that had become her guiding light:

1. Visualize the work
2. Limit work in progress
3. Manage flow
4. Make policies explicit
5. Implement feedback loops
6. Improve collaboratively, evolve experimentally

These weren't just rules for a project management system anymore. They were a philosophy for life, a lens through which she now viewed the world.

Sally sealed the envelope, a sense of gratitude washing over her. Kanban had given her more than just a way to manage work – it had given her a new way of thinking, a new way of approaching challenges, and a new appreciation for the power of continuous improvement.

As she placed the thank you note in her bag, ready to deliver to Chris tomorrow, Sally felt a sense of excitement about what the future held. The Kanban journey wasn't over – in many ways, it felt like it was just beginning. There would be new challenges to face, new processes to improve, and new heights of efficiency to reach.

But now, armed with her Kanban mindset and a team of fellow Kanban converts, Sally knew they were ready for whatever came their way. The flow would continue, the improvements would never stop, and the sticky notes... well, the sticky notes would keep on flowing across the board, one small step at a time, continuously moving them all towards a better, more organized, and more fulfilling future.

As she drifted off to sleep that night, Sally's dreams were filled with smoothly flowing Kanban boards, each sticky note a stepping stone on the path from chaos to clarity, from stress to satisfaction, from stagnation to continuous improvement. The Kanban mindset had truly become a part of her, shaping not just how she worked, but how she lived.

And she wouldn't have it any other way.

Manav's Thoughts:

In this final chapter, Sally reflects on the mindset shift that Kanban has brought to her and her team. An advanced concept that could help them continue evolving is the **Kanban Maturity Model (KMM)**. KMM is a framework that helps teams assess their current level of Kanban maturity and identify areas for improvement.

For Sally's team, using KMM could provide a roadmap for their ongoing evolution. By understanding their current level of Kanban maturity, they could set goals for continuous improvement, refine their processes, and further integrate Kanban into the company culture.

From a practical standpoint, KMM allows teams to track their progress over time and identify opportunities to deepen their Kanban practice. It also helps teams understand the stages of Kanban adoption and what's needed to move from one stage to the next.

For further reading on the Kanban Maturity Model, check out:

- "Kanban Maturity Model" by David J. Anderson & Teodora Bozheva
- "The Toyota Way to Lean Leadership: Achieving and Sustaining Excellence through Leadership Development" by Jeffrey K. Liker and Gary L. Convis

These resources explore how teams can continue to evolve and mature their Kanban practices over time, helping them achieve sustained success.

Epilogue

A Year in the Life of a Kanban Team

Sally leaned back in her chair, a satisfied smile playing on her lips as she looked at the large screen displaying their team's metrics. It had been exactly one year since they fully embraced Kanban, and the results were nothing short of remarkable.

"Hard to believe it's been a whole year, huh?" Chris said, appearing at her side with two steaming cups of coffee.

Sally accepted the coffee gratefully. "I know. Sometimes it feels like we've always worked this way, and other times I can't believe how far we've come."

As they sipped their coffee, Sally's mind wandered back to the chaotic days before Kanban. The constant firefighting, the missed deadlines, the stressed-out team members – it all seemed like a distant memory now.

"Hey team," Sally called out, "let's take a moment to celebrate our Kanban-versary!"

The team gathered around, curious to see the results of their year-long journey.

"Alright, folks," Sally began, pulling up a series of charts on the screen. "Let's look at some numbers, shall we?"

The first chart showed their cycle time over the past year. "Our average cycle time has decreased by 50%," Sally explained. "We're delivering value to our customers twice as fast as we used to."

Dave whistled appreciatively. "No wonder our customers have been so happy lately."

Sally nodded, moving to the next chart. "Speaking of happy customers, our customer satisfaction scores have increased by 35%. And look at this – our defect rate has dropped by 60%."

Tina from QA beamed with pride. "That's what happens when you build quality into the process instead of trying to test it in at the end!"

As Sally continued to share the impressive metrics – increased throughput, reduced work item age, improved predictability – she couldn't help but reflect on the journey that had brought them here.

"You know," she said, turning to the team, "these numbers are great, but they don't tell the whole story. I think what I'm most proud of is how we've grown as a team."

Chris nodded in agreement. "We've really embraced the spirit of continuous improvement. Remember when we started our Kanban cadences? Those regular strategy reviews and operations reviews seemed like overkill at first, but now they're the backbone of our improvement process."

"And don't forget about our explicit policies," Dave chimed in. "Having clear, agreed-upon rules for how we manage our work has been a game-changer. No more confusion about what 'done' means or how to handle blockers."

Sally smiled, remembering the heated discussions they'd had while establishing those policies. "It wasn't always easy, but it was worth it. And speaking of not easy, remember when we first started setting Service Level Expectations?"

The team groaned collectively, but with good humor.

"Oh boy, do I," Tina laughed. "We were way too optimistic at first. But you know what? Learning to set realistic expectations and then consistently meet them has done wonders for our relationship with stakeholders."

As the team continued to reminisce and celebrate their successes, Sally's phone buzzed with a message. It was from the CEO: "Great job on implementing Kanban in your team. How do you feel about scaling it up to the entire development department?"

Sally's eyes widened. She looked up at her team, then back at the message. "Hey Chris," she called out, "remember when we talked about Portfolio Kanban? I think we're about to get a crash course in scaling Kanban."

Chris grinned, always ready for a new challenge. "Bring it on. We've got the Kanban Maturity Model to guide us. We'll take it one level at a time."

As the team huddled around to hear about their new challenge, Sally felt a surge of excitement. They had come so far, but there was still so much to learn and improve.

"Alright, team," she said, her voice filled with determination. "We've mastered team-level Kanban. Now it's time to take it to the next level. Who's with me?"

The enthusiastic response from her teammates told her all she needed to know. They were ready for whatever came next.

Later that evening, as Sally updated her personal Kanban board (yes, she had one at home now too), she reflected on the lessons she'd learned over the past year. If she could give advice to someone just starting their Kanban journey, what would she say?

1. Start small, but think big. Begin with visualizing your work, then gradually introduce other Kanban principles.
2. Embrace the spirit of continuous improvement. Kanban is not a destination, it's a journey.
3. Make policies explicit. Clear rules reduce confusion and conflicts.
4. Use data to drive decisions. Metrics are your friends, but remember that not everything that matters can be measured.
5. Foster a culture of collaboration. Kanban works best when everyone is on board.
6. Be patient. Sustainable change takes time.
7. Don't forget about upstream and downstream processes. Optimizing your team's work is great, but consider how you can apply Kanban principles to your entire value stream.
8. Learn to manage risk. Use Kanban to identify potential issues early and address them proactively.
9. Celebrate your wins, learn from your failures. Both are valuable in the Kanban journey.
10. Remember that Kanban is adaptable. Make it work for you, not the other way around.

As she pinned these lessons to her board, Sally couldn't help but smile. The Kanban journey had transformed not just how she worked, but how she approached life itself. It had taught her to value flow over busyness, quality over quantity, and continuous improvement over perfection.

Tomorrow would bring new challenges – scaling Kanban, managing a portfolio of projects, perhaps even helping other departments start their own Kanban journeys. But Sally wasn't worried. She and her team had the tools, the mindset, and the experience to tackle whatever came their way.

As she got ready for bed, Sally glanced at her Kanban board one last time. In the 'To Do' column, a new sticky note caught her eye: "Write a book about our Kanban journey?"

She chuckled to herself. "Maybe someday," she murmured. "After all, in the world of Kanban, anything is possible."

With that thought, Sally turned off the lights, ready to rest and recharge for another day of continuous improvement. The Kanban adventure wasn't over. And she couldn't wait to see where it would take them next.

Manav's Thoughts:

First of all, congratulations on making it to the end of Sally's Kanban journey! You've just completed a significant step toward mastering the fundamentals of Kanban and, more importantly, embracing a mindset of continuous improvement. But as we know, the real beauty of Kanban lies in its ability to grow with us. Just as Sally and her team evolved, your Kanban journey is just getting started.

At this stage, you might be asking, "What's next?" Well, Kanban, like any methodology, offers an endless well of knowledge to explore. While this book has touched on many core and advanced concepts—ranging from work item types and WIP limits to more advanced topics like flow efficiency and risk management—there is always more to learn and apply. One of the strengths of Kanban is its flexibility and adaptability to new environments, industries, and challenges.

Maybe as you continue your own journey, you'll encounter new problems or scenarios that inspire curiosity. If that happens, I encourage you to embrace that curiosity. There are countless advanced concepts out there—like **Portfolio Kanban**, which deals with managing work across multiple teams or projects, or **Kanban for DevOps**, which emphasizes the synergy between Kanban and automation. These ideas and more could deepen your understanding and application of Kanban in even broader contexts.

If you come across any of these interesting concepts or have insights from your own experience with Kanban, I would love to hear from you! Don't hesitate to reach out and share your thoughts. Who knows? Your idea could be featured in the next edition of this book, and of course, I would be thrilled to give you full acknowledgment for your contribution.

I also want to take a moment to reflect on how far you've come. Not only have you journeyed with Sally through her team's transformation, but you've also explored the power of Kanban in your own professional or personal life. Remember, the principles of Kanban don't just apply to work; they can shape the way we approach all aspects of life, from planning personal projects to improving our daily routines.

My goal with this book was not just to teach you Kanban but to ignite a spark—a spark that makes you curious, makes you question how things work, and makes you want to continuously improve. This isn't the end; it's the first step of your Kanban journey. And I hope you carry this mindset of exploration and curiosity with you wherever you go.

Before I go, I'd like to thank you for taking the time to read this book and for joining me on this adventure. It has been an honor to share Sally's story with you, and I hope you found it engaging, insightful, and fun.

If you enjoyed this journey, I'd also love to hear from you about other topics or areas where you'd like to see similar story-driven approaches. Whether it's related to Agile, Scrum, leadership, or something completely different, I'm always eager to explore new ideas and create content that resonates with you. So don't hesitate to reach out—your input can shape the direction of future books, and together, we can continue learning and growing.

Thank you once again for being part of this journey. Let's continue striving for continuous improvement—both in our work and in life. Until next time, keep exploring, keep improving, and keep in touch.

Warm regards,
Manav

ABOUT THE AUTHOR

Manav Agarwal is an experienced Agile Transformation Leader and Coach with a passion for promoting agile mindsets in organizations. With a career spanning over a decade in the tech industry, Manav has established himself as a driving force in the agile community and is known for his innovative approaches to implementing Scrum and SAFe® in various environments.

With an engineer's mind and a teacher's heart, Manav's journey into the world of Agile began during his academic days at the prestigious IIT Bombay. There, he honed his skills in aerospace engineering while discovering his talent for breaking down complex concepts into easily understandable parts.

His thinking has been shaped by international experience, including a Masters in Project Management in France and studies at the University of Toronto in Canada. This multicultural background enables him to adapt agile principles to different cultural contexts, making him a versatile coach in the global business world.

His professional journey has taken him through renowned companies such as Airbus, Hager and Alten, where he has always proven his ability to lead teams, implement agile methods and drive digital transformations. But it was at Siemens where Manav found his true calling as an Agile Transformation Leader.

As a SAFe® Program Consultant (SPC) and PMI Agile Certified Practitioner (PMI-ACP®), Manav has trained and coached hundreds of professionals in agile methods and SAFe. His workshops are known for their hands-on and interactive approach, enriched with real-world anecdotes and a touch of humor - a skill he has perfected through his hobby of stand-up comedy.

In his role as an adult education trainer, Manav regularly conducts workshops on the agile mindset, reaching a wider audience by spreading the agile philosophy beyond the tech industry. His ability to combine technical expertise with soft skills makes his trainings both informative and transformative.

Manav's approach to agile coaching is holistic and people-centered. He believes that true agility goes beyond processes and tools - it's about fostering a mindset of continuous improvement, adaptability and collaboration. His experience in various industries - from aerospace to renewable energy - has given him unique insights into the application of agile principles in different contexts.

With his combination of technical expertise, teaching talent and infectious enthusiasm for all things agile, Manav continues to inspire and guide individuals and organizations on their agile transformation journey. His ultimate goal? To spread the agile mindset not only in IT teams, but throughout organizations and beyond to create a more adaptive, collaborative and innovative world.

BOOKS BY THIS AUTHOR

When Sally Met Agile

Beyond Frameworks: Tailoring Agile to Your World

Join Sally on a witty and insightful journey through the messy reality of Agile adoption. Blending storytelling and practical advice, this book helps you craft an Agile approach that truly fits your team.

When Sally Met Kanban

A Journey from Chaos to Clarity

Discover Kanban through Sally's workplace adventures as she learns how flow, focus, and small changes create lasting impact. With humor and real-world lessons, this story makes Kanban approachable and fun.

The Silent Whisper

Tales of Love in the AI Era

Step into Millbrook, a small town quietly transformed by artificial intelligence. Through interconnected stories of love, loss, and humanity, this collection explores what it means to be human in the age of algorithms.

www.ingramcontent.com/pod-product-compliance
Lightning Source LLC
Chambersburg PA
CBHW050303230526
45471CB00005B/1994